David Plante is the author of several novels, the most recent of which were the highly-acclaimed *The Country* and *The Woods*.

D0846881

Also by David Plante

THE GHOST OF HENRY JAMES
SLIDES
RELATIVES
THE DARKNESS OF THE BODY
FIGURES IN BRIGHT AIR
THE FAMILY
THE COUNTRY
THE WOODS

DAVID PLANTE

Difficult Women

a memoir of three

Futura
Macdonald & Co
London & Sydney

A Futura Book

Copyright © David Plante 1979, 1983

The memoir of Jean Rhys originally appeared, in
somewhat different form, in *The Paris Review*.

Thanks are due to the executors of the Estate of Jean Rhys
for permission to quote from her unpublished papers; a
portion of a letter from Sonia Orwell to the author is
quoted by permission of the Estate of the late Sonia
Brownell Orwell.

First published in Great Britain in 1983 by
Victor Gollancz Ltd

This Futura edition published in 1984

ISBN 0 7088 2450 1

Reproduced, printed and bound in Great Britain by
Hazell Watson & Viney Limited,
Member of the BPCC Group,
Aylesbury, Bucks

Futura Publications
A Division of
Macdonald & Co (Publishers) Ltd
Maxwell House
74 Worship Street
London EC2A 2EN
A BPCC plc Company

Contents

Contents

Jean

I ASKED AT reception for Mrs Hamer. It always gave me pleasure to use her married name, not the name she was known by. She once told me some of the names she had used in her life to keep her life secret, and I forgot them. To refer to her as Mrs Hamer, which was a private name, and not as Jean Rhys, meant, I suppose, that I was a part of her private world, the world she wanted to remain forever her world. I wondered why I should want to be a part of it.

The receptionist, an old woman with lank hair, looked at the register. Behind her was a mirror and on either side of the mirror were white glass shells with lights inside. She said, "I don't think we have a Mrs Hamer." I said, "Jean Rhys." "Yes," she said, "she's waiting in the pink lounge."

I was carrying a bottle of wine. The carpet of the pink lounge was patterned with large soft pink roses on a grey background. The wallpaper was pink. The floor lamps, lit, had great dark pink shades. Jean was sitting at the corner of a red sofa, under a lamp; she wore a wide-brimmed pink hat. Her head was lowered, her fist up to her chin, and she was staring at the floor, her blue eyes bulging a little. She did not look up as I approached.

I said, "Jean."

With a sudden jolt of her small, hunched body, as if I had frightened her, she dropped her hand and raised her head to look at me. "Oh David," she said, "I can't tell you how happy I am to see you."

I put the bottle of wine on the little table before the sofa and kissed her. "You're looking marvellous," I said.

"Don't lie to me," she said. "I'm dying."

I sat on the couch by her.

"Can I ask you something?" she said. "Will you go and buy me

a bottle of sweet vermouth? They don't have any in this hotel."
She laughed, a small ha, that lifted her shoulders. "It's that kind of
hotel." She looked about, as with sudden suspicion, and gave
another small shrugging laugh. "A big dreary hotel in South
Kensington filled with old people whom they won't allow to
drink sweet vermouth."

On another red sofa across the room, and in big red armchairs,
were old people, men and women, their canes held alongside
them or between their legs; none were talking, and some were
asleep.

When I went out quickly to an off-licence it occurred to me the
day was bright, and I was very aware, when I came back to the
hotel, of the grey interior, and all the lights lit with dim bulbs. I
ordered glasses and ice from a waiter with satin lapels and a
crooked black bow tie.

As I poured out the drinks on a table before us, Jean sat back and
crossed her legs. Her body seemed bent in many ways; she had to
grab one leg and heft it across the other, and, once crossed, you
thought she could never uncross them. I gave her a drink and she
smiled. As she drank she pulled at the brim of her hat.

This was December 1975. I hadn't seen her in a year, since the
last time she had come up to London for a few weeks.

"Now," she said, "give me your news. I hope it's cheerful."

I tried to make my news entertaining; she listened, drinking
and pulling at her hat, her large clear blue eyes staring attentively
at me. Sometimes she laughed.

"Now," she said, "I'll tell you my news."

She prepared herself by taking a drink.

"Well," she said, "I got a letter from the tax people. They said I
hadn't paid my taxes. I got very upset. I thought I had. I'd sent
everything off to my accountant, as he'd told me to. But a tax
man came to the house and said I had to pay my taxes. I said I'd
written to my accountant, but he said that didn't matter, I had to
pay. I said I couldn't. He said, 'I'm only here on orders.' I said,
'That's what the fascists used to say.' He left angry. The next day
I got a letter saying if I didn't pay my taxes they'd take my house
away from me. I rang up my accountant. He said, 'Oh, they're
always threatening to do things like that.' But I was worried. I
was so worried, I fell. I've been dying ever since."

"I hate tax people," I said.

She bared her teeth. "Hate them," she said. "I know what they do. I know." She snorted. "Fascists!" Her drink splashed over her glass. "They take what I have and put it in their pockets." I wondered if she were joking, and I laughed; but her face twisted a little, and she bared her teeth again and said, "They've taken over the world." Then she looked at her drink. "Well, I'll be dead soon. They won't be able to get anything more from me." She drank.

I said, "The fact is I don't understand much about taxes, and—"

"Neither do I. I never did. I never understood anything that had to do with mathematics and machines, so I never understood more than half of what goes on in the world."

A thin young woman with black hair and dressed in black came into the pink lounge. She went to a window and drew closed the grey draperies over the net curtains, making the lounge dimmer. At her appearance, a number of old people, clutching their canes for support, began to rise.

Jean said, "That's the manageress. When she appears, everyone rises."

"Why?"

"She doesn't exactly announce it, but they know that when she comes in lunch is being served."

I sat with Jean as the old people followed the manageress out of the lounge into the dining room.

She said, "All those old people, all alone."

I looked at them.

Jean said, "This is a horrible hotel."

"It is a bit grim."

"Well," she said, "we'd better go in. The manageress will be annoyed if we're late. Will you give me my stick?"

I gave her first her handbag, then her silver-topped stick, which she used to steady herself as I helped her up with my hand under her arm. She was surprisingly heavy, and dropped back. I got her to her feet, held her arm, picked up the bottle of wine from the table, and supported her as we walked slowly to the dining room.

She said, "Let's pretend you're my son. That'll cheer me up."

A waiter opened the bottle of wine while Jean and I studied the menu. She was wearing her glasses, got from her handbag; the lenses were so smeared I wondered how she saw through them. We both ordered curried eggs. She put the glasses back in her handbag. The waiter poured out the wine.

There was a smell of mould in the dining room. My napkin was almost wet.

With one glass of wine Jean began to giggle as she talked. I could only get words, as she held her hands, sometimes her napkin, to her mouth while she talked. Whenever she giggled I smiled. Her hands were as if disjointed at the knuckles.

With more wine, she ceased giggling. I still didn't understand most of what she said, which, spoken in a soft grave voice, seemed to me jumbled. She tugged more and more at her hat brim, pulled her hair, and rubbed her forehead, and I understood that what she was talking about was making her somewhat frantic. I heard: "The world . . . awful it is . . . gone *phut* . . . want out, that's all . . . taken over . . . not understanding, anyone . . ." She held out her glass to be refilled.

As her hands were shaky, her makeup was hit-and-miss; there were patches of thick beige powder on her jaw and on the side of her nose, her lipstick was as much around her lips as on them, the marks of the eye pencil criss-crossed her lids, so I thought she might easily have jabbed it in her eyes. But the eyes were very clear and blue and strong, and the angles of her cheekbones sharp.

She put her hands to her mouth, laughed, and her eyes went bright: I didn't know what she was laughing about.

We had baked apples for pudding, but she left most of hers. She said, throwing her napkin down, "Thank God that's over. Now we can go up to my room for a drink."

Getting Jean up to her room was difficult. She leaned on me so heavily I at times lost balance. We lurched from piece of furniture to piece of furniture, wall to wall, she with her hand extended to lean for a moment before we continued. Sometimes her cane got caught between her legs, and I had to straighten it. Getting her into the lift I had to twist my body, it seemed, in many directions at the same time. I could not imagine how she had got down to the lounge from her room. She leaned her small hunched back against the passage wall and sighed as I opened the door to her room with her key.

The room was all pink. There were two beds; a lamp, with a big pink shade, was on a table between the beds. Jean, in her pink hat, sat on the first bed. She threw her cane down and closed her eyes; after a moment she opened her eyes wide, shook her head, and said, "Never mind."

"Never mind what?" I asked.

She laughed. "Let's have a drink," she said.

"What will you have?"

"Rum." She tried to rise by pressing her hands on the bed. "But I want to sit on a chair."

I helped her to one of the two red-brown chairs before a window with net curtains and red-brown draperies. She, as she would have said, "collapsed" into the chair.

I went to the desk where the drinks bottles and glasses were on a tray.

"The manageress won't let us have ice," she said.

"That's ridiculous. Of course we'll have ice." I rang for some. She did not seem impressed or in any way proved wrong when the ice came; she might have thought the ice came because I was a man.

I said, "Jean, there's no rum here."

"No rum? Did you want rum?"

"No. You asked for it."

"Did I?" She passed her hand over her forehead. "That's strange, I must have thought I was in Dominica, where of course you'd have rum. But it's so long since I've been in Dominica. I'll have a gin and vermouth. And please don't put too much ice in. *They* fill the glass with ice so I won't drink too much. Well, why shouldn't I?"

I thought: Yes, why shouldn't she? I gave her a big drink. I took a smaller one, lit a lamp in the dim room, and sat on the other chair.

"When were you last in Dominica?" I asked.

"Oh, years and years ago, on a visit. But I left when I was sixteen to come to England, and the visit later made me see that I could never go back to the island I knew as a girl. It was beautiful. It was so beautiful. When I went back I found all the rivers—you know, there are three hundred and sixty-five rivers in Dominica, one for every day of the year—all were polluted. I used to drink from them when I was a girl. Gone, all gone. And who's responsible? Who?" She crossed her legs. "I know, I know." She snorted a little. "Yeah. I know."

I didn't know, and I didn't know if I should ask her. I said, "Who?"

She stared at me. "You're liberal, aren't you? I'm surrounded by liberals. You don't understand what's happening. *They're* taking over. Yeah. I know. I used to be liberal. No more."

I said, "I thought you told me you were once a communist."

She laughed; her thin yellow teeth showed. "I was a G.K. Chesterton sort of socialist, a cow and an acre of land for every man, that kind of thing. No." She threw up one hand; the other held the glass. "Anyway, honey, I'll be dead before they take over."

I said, "We'll fight them together."

"Will we?"

"Sure," I said, though I wasn't sure what we were fighting.

She pulled her hat brim and leaned forward. She said, "I'm going to tell you something."

I smiled at her.

"I'm going to tell you how I started to write."

I kept my smile, a smile, I recognize now, I always kept when she told me something that interested me very much, but which I did not want her to think I had in any way solicited from her. Perhaps one of the reasons I was with her was to hear how she started to write; but the moment she was about to tell me, I wasn't sure I wanted to hear, or wasn't sure I wanted her to think I did.

"Do you want to hear?" she asked.

"Of course I do."

"Maybe," she said, "you'll write it down. I can't now. I can't write. It'll never be written. I'll tell you, and you write it down."

"All right."

"Give me another drink first, honey."

I gave her another big drink.

Jean, I think, often prepared what she was going to say to you before you arrived, and when she told you she made it seem as if she had suddenly thought of it.

"When I was little I heard voices in my head that had nothing to do with me. I sometimes didn't even know the words. But they wanted to be written down, so I wrote them down. Well, there it is. Some time after, a long time after, but still a long time ago, oh a long time ago, before the First World War—" She took a drink. "People say about him he was a villain. He wasn't. People don't understand. He was kind to me. He was kind to me when I had no one else to help me. And if he left me after the abortion, well—" She shrugged. "I lived afterwards in a bed-sitter in Holborn. I had so little money. If you had an evening gown at that time, that was all you needed to get into the crowd scene of a film. I made a little money that way. But not enough, not enough for the landlord. When I paid the first week's rent I was surprised to see how little money I had left. I sat in the armchair looking out of the window on to the empty street. London is always empty at Christmas. The landlord knocked. He came in with a Christmas tree, about three feet high, with candles and silver paper and a star at the top, and he put it on the table and said, 'Very pretty,' and went out. And there was money. I thought, I can't take this, I can't take this—" Jean looked down at the floor, her lower lip drew up as if she had just tasted something very sour, and she began to cry; the tears ran down her nose. It took her a long time to continue, and when she did her voice was higher. "But I thought, I need it, I need it. So I kept it. And after that I didn't care, it didn't matter—"

She paused again, her face contorted; the tears flowed down her nose and cheeks, and when she wiped them away with the sides of her crooked hands, her makeup streaked. I reached out and put my hand on her arm. She looked at me, weeping and, I thought, pleading with me. I said, "I'll get you a tissue." I went into the bathroom, pulled a tissue out of a box, brought it back to her. She put her drink down, wiped her eyes, blew her nose. She sat still.

"When I met someone else, I jumped at him. He wanted me to marry him. I said yes. His name was Jean. I went to Holland to marry him. I didn't know much about him, about what work he did. I had, do you know?, a Japanese passport for a while. That was the only passport Jean could get, so I, as his wife, got one too." She suddenly laughed, her face immediately shifting from one expression to another; she opened her mouth and "ha, ha, ha" came out from between her teeth, and her blue eyes were wide and bright. "When I came back to England with my Japanese passport, they stopped me, they said, 'You don't look Japanese.'"

With a hand reaching as if uncertainly into darkness, she reached for her drink. "The man I had for so long been dependent on met me. He took me to the Piccadilly Grill. It was smart then. He said, 'I want you to know that Jean's a spy, I'm warning you.' I said, 'I don't care.' I didn't. Nothing mattered. That was in 1919, after the war." She drank and pulled at the brim of her hat and pulled the hair that came out on her forehead back under the hat; she pulled again at the brim.

'Anyway, I gave the Christmas tree away; took a taxi to a hospital for sick children and gave it away, then went back to my room, and I thought, well, I know what I'll do. I'll wait till the landlord goes out, till the house is empty. Plenty of time. I smoked half a pack of cigarettes and looked at the bottle of gin on the table. I hated gin. Someone knocked on the door. It was a girl from one of the crowd scenes of the old-time movies. She immediately saw what I was planning to do. She didn't tell me not to. She said, 'You won't kill yourself if you jump out the window, you'll just maim yourself. You don't want to be a vegetable for the rest of your life, do you?'" Jean laughed. "I said, 'No, no, I don't want to be a vegetable, not me.' So we drank the bottle of gin. I hated gin then. I don't know why I bought it. Maybe I didn't buy it, but found it in a cupboard. Now, I drink gin and sweet vermouth. Maybe I should change my drink. I think I should change my life entirely. I'm going to give up on my life. That's what I'm going to do. I'm indifferent. I'm indifferent, even, to passion. I don't care. I'll wear red slacks, a shabby silk blouse, and a red wig. Anyway, who cares? No one cares." She drank. "She brought me some Turkish slippers as a Christmas gift, bought them in a market. She didn't know my size, but they fit. That was nice of her. We drank the gin. I don't know where that came from. This is all so unimportant. Who cares?

"Well," I said, "I do."

"Do you? Sometimes I think you only pretend that you do."

"You're going to have to take my word for it," I said. "And if I didn't care I could make an excuse and leave."

She shrugged. "You could."

I waited as she stared at the floor. Then she remembered her drink.

"She said to me—I can't recall her name. I liked her rather. We were in a party scene together in the movie. We had to pretend we were talking together and having a good time. She said, 'Why don't you move out of this dreary room?' Would she have used the word 'dreary'? I don't know. She said, 'Why don't you move to Chelsea? There are a lot of sugars there.'"

"Sugar daddies?" I asked.

"Sugars," she said. "Yeah. Sugars. I never thought of him as a sugar, though I guess he was."

"Who?"

She looked at me as if amazed that I should ask. "The first one," she said.

"Oh yes," I said.

"They misunderstand him. He used to ask me about Dominica, about the flowers and the birds. They say we treated the blacks badly there. We didn't. And who has ruined the island? Who has polluted the rivers? He listened to me talk. He was patient. Maybe I do have black blood in me. I think my great-grandmother was coloured, the Cuban. She was supposed to be a Vatican countess. I think she was coloured. Where else would I get my love for pretty clothes? And oh how I envied them, in their clothes, dancing in the street. But what have they done to Dominica? What? It's all gone. I don't ever want to go back. No, never, never. He understood me—a little. I don't know if Jean understood me."

"Your husband?" I asked.

She seemed not quite sure whom I was referring to, as though I had introduced a character from outside the story. "My husband?"

"Didn't you say you married Jean?"

"I married him. I went to Holland to marry him, after the war. I took the first boat I could get on. I didn't care. I didn't know what he did exactly, I still don't know. From Holland we went to Paris. That was lovely, Paris. We lived in a hotel, and sat out on the balcony and drank white wine." She stared at me. "You know," she said, "I had a son who was born in Paris."

"A son?"

"Did you know?"

I wondered if she thought I might have had some access to the story of her life which she didn't know about—and of course I did: her novels. She did not, however, think that in reading her novels one knew anything about her life.

"No," I said.

"I came back to the hotel room with it, from the hospital. It slept in a cot in a corner. One day the *sage femme* came from the hospital to look at it. She said, 'I think your child has to go back to the hospital.' I said, 'You think so?' She took it away. I got a *bleu* a little while later to say it was dying and did I want it baptized? I asked Jean. He said, 'No, never, I won't have a child of mine baptized.' I became upset. He went out and bought some champagne; we drank the champagne and I felt better. The next morning I got another *bleu* saying my son had died. I wondered if it died while we were drinking champagne."

"What did it die of?" I asked.

'*Je n'sais pas*," she said. "I must have done something wrong. I was never a good mother."

I didn't say anything.

"After Paris we went to Vienna. But I don't want to talk about Vienna."

"You wrote a story called 'Vienne'."

"Yes," she said, "I did. I bought some pretty clothes in Vienna. Then everything went wrong. All wrong. Anyway, give me another drink, honey."

I put a lot of ice in the drink and very little gin in the vermouth.

She raised her glass to me. "Here's to you."

"Here's to you," I said, and raised my glass.

"No, not me. I don't matter. I never did, much. I don't now."

"That's not true."

"It is. It is true. I don't matter, and I want out." She looked at her drink as she brought it to her mouth. She said, "You put a lot of ice in this."

"It'll melt," I said.

"That's what they all say," she said.

I sat by her.

"It wasn't exactly Chelsea," she said. "It was more Fulham.

And the room looked exactly like the one I had left in Holborn. I didn't meet any sugars. And I couldn't forget him. You see," she said, "I had to keep accepting money from him. I got used to that. I didn't see him. The money was sent through his solicitor. I took the money. I didn't care." Her face contorted, and tears rose to her eyes as she looked at me. "I don't care about anything any more. I know how to do it now. Not jumping out a window. Not taking pills, because they just pump out your stomach." She stuck out her jaw. "No, I've got it all plotted out. And I won't tell anyone. Not even you." She paused and stared at me; her crying was making her eyes swell. "I'm boring you."

"You're not."

"I know I am. I am a bore. But it doesn't matter, it doesn't matter. Nothing matters, my work less than anything."

I said, "Jean—," wondering how reasonably to reassure her.

Startling me, she suddenly stuck out her thin neck and shouted, "Oh what a Goddamn shitty business we've taken on, being writers! Oh what shit! What shit!" She shook her head, with its hat, whenever she said "shit", as if to shake the word out with physical disgust. I had never heard her use the word before. "I'm over eighty." She had never revealed her age before. "Look at me. And what have I done? Nothing! Nothing! Mediocrity. Mediocre, that's what my work is. And these stories they want me to publish. Not good. I don't want to publish them. I've wasted two and a half years on them. I wanted to write about my life. I wanted to write my autobiography, because everything they say about me is wrong. I want to tell the truth. I want to tell the truth, too, about Dominica. No, it's not true we treated the black people badly. We didn't, we didn't. Now they say we did. No, no. I'm becoming a fascist. They won't listen. No one listens."

"I'm listening," I said.

"Oh yes, you," she said, as though I *would* listen. "I remember a black man in Dominica walking through the yard. My father and I were on the back steps of the house. My father made me give loaves of French bread—Dominica was once French and the bread was still in long loaves—and sixpence to poor black men who came to us. No women ever came. I recall this black man walking away from us, the loaf under his arm, and his dignity. His dignity and his unconquerable mind. Do you believe it?"

I asked, "What's that, Jean?" I was suddenly speaking, it seemed to me, from a great remoteness.

"You don't know?"

"No."

"'Live and take comfort . . . thou hast great allies; thy friends are exultations, agonies, and love, and man's unconquerable mind.'"

"I don't recognize it," I said.

"Fancy you don't know it. That's maybe because you're American. Americans are so stupid. They don't know anything, only their own literature, which isn't much. We're friends, aren't we? You've got to forget about all past American writers. You've got to forget about Henry James. You've got to forget about America. 'Live and take comfort . . . thou hast great allies; thy friends are exultations, agonies, and man's unconquerable mind—'" She put her glass down, her hands to her face; when she took her hands away her face was wet and twisted with weeping. "'—and man's unconquerable mind'." She raised her hands. "Oh, to die like a tree falling. Oh, to be big, to be large, to be huge. That's what you have to be. To be big. There are no big people in the world now. You must be big." She picked up her drink, paused, then whispered, in sing-song, "'Oh England, my England, what can I do for you?' No, that's wrong. 'What can I do for you, oh England, my England?'" Her face tensed. She spat. "It's shit. It's shit, England."

Her face became smooth, her eyes went out of focus. "And yet, and yet. Nelson, he was big. There were big people in England. He was like a Caesar. 'Kiss me, Hardy.' He wasn't homosexual, I don't believe it. He was bisexual, as we all are. He was big, was great, was huge. He died for England. England? 'What can I do for you, oh England, my England?' I came here when I was sixteen, to this cold dark country, where I was never warm." Her upper lip rose and she again spat. "Shit!"

Immediately, her face relaxed again, became, it seemed, as soft and vague as her eyes. "And yet, I do know it had a certain gentleness, an honesty. Gone, all gone. In the West Country, there you can still find people who are like trees, and when they die they die like huge trees falling over. People close to the land. I'll never, never forget the dignity of that black man walking through the yard with his sixpence and the loaf of bread under his arm. And it's all gone, all gone. They've destroyed it themselves. Are there any men now like that black man? We didn't treat them badly, we didn't. They say we did. It's all gone, the dignity, and I want out. There are no big men left." She shouted, "War! War! War! Martyrs, and for what? For what? There was a boy from the West Country, died in Belfast. He was nineteen. He wanted to be a sailor. Oh they killed him, they killed him! I remember, during the war, I worked in a canteen in King's Cross, serving breakfast to soldiers who were going across. We weren't allowed, the girls, to get into conversations with the soldiers. We served them, that was all. There was one, a young soldier, belted up with all kinds of straps and tin cans hanging from the straps, who came behind the counter into the kitchen. He must have done it on a dare. He said he had a strap twisted and would I straighten it for him? I did, and he gave me a big wink. And I wondered for a long time if he died. Oh war! It's all gone. I wanted to tell you how I started to write. I'm telling you. I'll never write it now that I'm telling you. Will you write it? If you don't, it doesn't matter. Nothing matters, nothing matters. It's all shit." She laughed. "I'm a slut without a penny." Her face twisted and she wept. "Nothing matters. Nothing." She laughed again, with a shrug of her body, and, in a very quiet voice, sang:

> "If you want to be happy,
> Like a child with a toy balloon,
> Turn your money over in your pocket
> In the light of a full moon."

She shook her head and drank. "'Man's unconquerable mind'. Fancy you don't know that. 'Upon this bank and shoal of time, I'll leap to time to come.' Do you know that?"

I half frowned, half smiled. "Let me think—"

"You don't know. It's because you're American, and Americans are stupid. You should know. You should know it all. You should know all the big writers, the big big writers." She raised her hand. "You have to be big." She lowered her hand. "And yet, and yet, I'm so small, I'm nothing."

"Jean," I said, "please—" I did not know how to respond to

her. When she laughed, I smiled; when she wept, I stared sadly at her. Sometimes, because her feelings changed so quickly, I stared when she laughed, and smiled when she wept.

She said, "Listen to me. I want to tell you something very important. All of writing is a huge lake. There are great rivers that feed the lake, like Tolstoy and Dostoevsky. And there are trickles, like Jean Rhys. All that matters is feeding the lake. I don't matter. The lake matters. You must keep feeding the lake. It is very important. Nothing else is important."

Tears came to my eyes.

"Do you believe that?" she asked.

"Yes."

"But you now should be taking from the lake before you can think of feeding it. You must dip your bucket in very deep."

I blinked to rid my eyes of tears.

"Oh David, oh, what one could do, what one could do! Not I. I can't do anything. I don't matter. What matters is the lake. And man's unconquerable mind."

I reached out and held her wrist for a moment.

She asked, "Do you hate women?"

I took my hand away.

"No," I said, "I don't hate women. I have very complicated feelings towards them."

"You must hate them, though."

"Sometimes I hate some women," I said.

"A man needs a woman," she said, "but a woman without a man is nothing, nothing."

"You really think that?"

"Yes. Yes, I do. What they try to make of me, women, I hate. I hate it. Do they understand? No. Does anyone understand? I hate. I hate them. We didn't treat them badly. We didn't. I hate them." She put her hand to her chin. "And yet I was kissed once by a Nigerian, in a café in Paris, and I understood, a little. I understand why they are attractive. It goes very deep. They danced, danced in the sunlight, and how I envied them." She stopped, appeared to collapse inwardly, her drink resting on her crossed leg; then she seemed suddenly to rouse herself internally, and she shouted, "Oh David, I'm unhappy. You be happy. I'm so unhappy, all my life I've been so unhappy. It's unfair. I'm dying. I want to die. It's unfair. I'm dying, my body's dying, and inside I think: it's unfair, it's unfair, I've never lived, I've never lived." She sank back and finished her drink. "But I don't care any more. I'm not even interested in makeup any more.

> "If you want to be happy
> Like a child with a toy balloon,
> Just turn your money in your pocket
> In the light of a new moon.

"Give me another drink, will you, honey? And put only one cube in it."

I did. I took another for myself; but, attentive and in my attentiveness frightened of Jean, I didn't get drunk.

She said, "I wanted to tell you how I started to write. I was living in Holborn. I hated it, the bed-sitting room. A girl friend came. No, she wasn't a girl friend. We were in a movie together. I can't remember her name. She said, 'Move to Chelsea. You'll have a good time in Chelsea. You'll get over him there.' I moved, not to Chelsea, but to Fulham, into a room that was exactly like the one I left. I was going to my room one day and I saw in a shop window some quills, red and green and blue, and I thought, how pretty, I'll buy some quill pens to liven up my grim little room. I went into the shop. I didn't know why, but I bought a copybook, too, a thick copybook with shiny black covers and a red edge. I bought, too, nibs, a blotter, ink. When I got back to my room I put everything on a table. I swear, I swear I didn't know what I was about to do until the palms of my hands began to tingle and I knew, all at once, that I was going to write, I was going to write in the copybook everything that had happened to me, that had happened between him and me, and I started then. I wrote for days."

In my mind I tried to put together the bits she told me. In one way I was bored and thought: She's right, none of this matters. And in another way I thought: I must get all this put together.

I said, "Then you met Jean?"

"Jean?"

"The man you married after you were abandoned."

"Abandoned? Did I say I was abandoned?"

"No. I said it."

She said, "I filled the copybook and I put it under my under-

clothes in the back of a drawer. When I went to Holland to marry
Jean I packed it. I packed it, over and over, every time we moved,
and we moved about a lot. Anyway—" She closed her eyes
slowly, as if she were very tired.

I said, "Would you like to rest now, Jean?"

She opened her eyes, as if surprised. "Don't go now, honey.
Stay. But maybe you want to go."

"No," I said, "I want to stay."

"How can you like listening to me talk on and on?"

I said, "I used to listen to my mother—"

The corner of her upper lip rose and her face took on the
hardness of an old whore who, her eyes red with having wept for
so long, suddenly decides to be hard. "Your mother?" she
snapped. "I don't want to hear about your mother!"

I shut up. I thought: What am I doing here, listening to her? Is it
because she is a writer? I am not sure I have read all her books, not
even sure I admire her very greatly as a novelist. Is it because I
want to know her so well that I will know her better than anyone
else, or know at least secrets she has kept from everyone else,
which I will always keep to myself? If so, why?

She said, pulling her hat brim so it now hung unevenly about
her head, "Jean and I lived in Paris. We lived in a hotel. We had a
daughter. We didn't have any money. I suggested to Jean that he
write some articles and I would translate them. I remembered
that I had met in London the wife of a newspaper correspondent,
that she now lived with him in Paris, and that she might help me.
I took the articles to her. She said she couldn't use them. Then, I
suppose when she saw the desperation on my face, she asked me if
I wrote anything. I said, at first, no. But, I don't know why, I
remembered the copybook I had filled up with writing years
before. I told her about it. She said she wanted to see it. I went
home, I wrapped it in newspaper, and left it with her concierge,
and I thought, well, that's the last of that. She got in touch with
me. She asked me if she could type it out and alter it, and I said
yes. I didn't know what she saw in it. She called it 'Triple Sec'.
She asked me if she could send it to Ford Madox Ford. I didn't
know who he was. She said, 'He runs a review, the *transatlantic
review*, and he's very famous for spotting good young writers
and helping them.' Well, she sent it." Jean raised her arm and let

her hand fall into her lap. "And that's how I got to know Ford."

With the mention of his name, I became more attentive, and more, I think, frightened. Here Jean was talking to me about this most private episode, the episode about which, she had said in her only references to it, so many people had told lies, lies, lies. It was as if she suddenly opened the door to the closed centre of her life, a café in Paris in the Twenties, and in the café were Jean and Ford and his wife Stella at one table, and at other tables were Hemingway, Gertrude Stein and Alice B. Toklas, and half-blind James Joyce. It was the café I had, since my adolescence, fantasized about sitting in. She was going to take me in and give me a seat by her in the café. I thought, staring at her: You are attentive to her, not as Mrs Hamer, but Jean Rhys; you are not really interested in the private life of Mrs Hamer, but very much in that of Jean Rhys. It is because she is a writer that you see her, sit with her, listen to her; your interest in her is literary. Her head was tilted and she was looking at me. You want to know her secrets because they have to do with Jean Rhys, the writer.

I said, "Jean, I think I should go."

She said, wistfully, her eyes large, "Do you, honey?"

"I should."

She smiled. Her eyes went out of focus. She said, "You've cheered me up."

"I'm glad."

"Sit with me for one more drink."

I had been with her, I saw from my watch, for five hours.

"One more," I said.

"I promise I won't bore you."

"You don't bore me."

I gave her another drink. She reached for it with both hands. Her makeup had streaked down her face with her crying, and her hair, which she had been pulling at, stuck out stiffly under the warped hat brim. Her eyes and nose were red.

She said, "Tell me about yourself."

"I'd much rather hear about you."

"You would say that,"

I laughed. I said, "Quote me some more lines of poetry."

She laughed, too. "You like that?"

"Yes."

She rubbed her forehead. "'. . . man's unconquerable mind',"
she said.

"Because I'm an American and inveterately stupid," I said,
"tell me who wrote that."

She frowned a little, as if it were an embarrassment to say
something so obvious. "Wordsworth."

"Which bit?"

"To Toussaint l'Ouverture, the black man who governed Santo
Domingo and led the free slaves—"

"I see," I said.

When she drank, the drink spilled down the side of her chin on
to her dress; she did not seem aware. It was as if she had to look all
over the room to find me before she could stare at me and say,
"I'll die soon." Her eyes narrowed on me. "I'll die without
having lived." A sneer came over her face, and I had the uncomfortable feeling that she was sneering at me. She said, with the
sneer, "'Upon this bank and shoal of time, I'll leap to time to
come.'" Her head wobbled. "Yes, yes, I'll leap. I want out." She
leaned towards me. "You don't understand. You never understood. I want out. I never wanted to be a writer. Never. I couldn't
help it. All I wanted was to be happy."

I put my glass down on the table between us. I said, "Jean,
excuse me."

She slumped back.

I got up, went, moving carefully about the furniture, to the
bathroom just off her room. I peed, washed my face. I looked at
myself in the mirror above the wash-basin and thought: Who are
you? When I came out, I thought Jean had died; slumped, she was
utterly motionless, her eyes wide open and blank. I stood over
her, said, "Jean," and her body, it appeared, was shocked into
attention to me; she looked up at me, and after a while, in a
slurred voice, said, "I know, you've got to go."

"I really have got to," I said.

"Before you go," she said, "help me to the toilet."

It took a lot of manoeuvering to get her up and into the
bathroom; I left her, her hat still on, holding to the wash-basin. In
her room, I walked about. There were vases of flowers on the
bureau, with cards. I thought: She's been in there a long time. I
heard: "Oh my God!", and it occurred to me that she had seen her

face in the mirror. I waited more, a longer while. I heard her say, "David, David." I went to the bathroom door, leaned close to it, and called, "Jean." There was no response. "Jean," I called. She said, in a weak voice, "Help me." I thought: But I can't go in. What does she want me for in there? "Help me," she said.

I opened the door a little, imagining, perhaps, that if I opened it only a little, only a little would have happened. I saw Jean, her head with the battered hat leaning far to the side, her feet, with the knickers about her ankles, just off the floor, stuck in the toilet. I had, I immediately realized, forgotten to lower the seat after I had peed. Jean said, with a kind of moan, "Help me." Her eyes were huge. She was clasping her raised knees. I stepped into the puddle of pee all around the toilet, put my arms around her, and lifted her. In my arms, she sobbed. I held her closely, but I was frightened to hold her too closely because she felt so frail, and I thought I might hurt her. Her body shook as she sobbed. The brim of her hat was under my chin; with one hand I took off her hat, put it on the wash-basin, and, holding Jean, kissed her on her forehead. I held her till she stopped sobbing.

I said, "Shall I try to carry you to the bed or can you walk?"

"I'll try to walk," she said.

But she was hobbled by her knickers. I leaned her against a wall, bent down, asked her to lift one foot then the other, and took off her sopping knickers. We walked small step by small step to the bed. I turned her round so she could sit on the foot, and she dropped backwards. She couldn't raise herself to lie full length. I drew her up by holding her under her arms and pulling slowly, but she was very heavy; the bedspread rucked under her. I finally got her full length. She was shivering. She said, "I'm so cold." I took a blanket from the second bed and covered her. She rolled her head back and forth against the pillow, and, weeping, said, "It doesn't matter. It doesn't matter. Nothing matters." Tears came from her nose as from her eyes; she tried to sniff them back. Her entire face, swollen and red, was wet. She wailed, "Nothing matters. Nothing matters."

I thought: What shall I do?

I said, "Jean, I must go out for a moment. I'll be back, I promise."

She didn't answer.

In the hotel lobby, my hand shaking, I rang the only person I knew of who could help, Sonia Orwell. She had in fact first introduced me to Jean some years before. I said to Sonia, "Jean seems to be having an attack." She said she would be there in fifteen minutes. I went back to Jean, who was still moaning, "It doesn't matter," but quietly.

Sonia came, said severely, "For God's sake, David, don't you know when someone's drunk?"

She told me to leave Jean to her now.

The next morning I rang Sonia. I said, "I want Jean to know I wasn't embarrassed and I hope she wasn't."

Sonia laughed. She said, "I'm putting Jean in another hotel. Give her a day or two to recover, then visit her. But, please, remember to lower the toilet seat next time."

She was staying now in a suite in a lovely small hotel off the Portobello Road. The windows at the back gave on a garden with big bare trees. Jean, wearing a long blue dressing gown, was sitting in a beautiful chair in the middle of the sitting room.

She said, "Now, David, if that ever happens to you with a lady again, don't get into a panic. You put the lady on her bed, cover her, put a glass of water and a sleeping pill on the bedside table, turn the lights down very low, adjust your tie before you leave so you'll look smart, say at reception that the lady is resting, and when you tell the story afterwards you make it funny."

I ordered glasses and ice. A young man with a long gold earring, white hair, and a suit that looked as though made of black plastic, came in with a tray; he placed the tray on a low table by Jean and kissed her, said, "Darling, blue has to be your favourite colour, it suits you so," and Jean, giggling, said, "I never wear green, that's an unlucky colour for me." The young man made the drinks for us.

Jean raised her glass to me and smiled; I raised mine to her.

She was, I realized, happy: she was wearing a pretty dressing gown in a pretty room. One of the signs of Jean's happiness, I came to realize, was her sadness; happy, she allowed herself to be, at least a little, sad. When she was really unhappy, she was angry. She had been unhappy at the hotel in Kensington; instead, however, of taking a practical step to change the hotel, even to asking for another to be found for her, she simply raged, as though nothing could be done and all she could do was rage. Now, in another hotel, she smiled a little sadly when I told her she was looking beautiful.

She said, "Wouldn't what happened to us make a funny story? We should write it."

I was somewhat amazed that she should so quickly think of turning the episode into a story; but I was excited, too. "Yes, let's," I said. An uncomfortable feeling came over me which I didn't recognize then, but which I now do: a feeling as of stealing manuscripts or letters from Jean, though she was allowing me to steal them, a feeling of some presumption, because *of course* I would be tempted to steal manuscripts and letters, *of course* I would want to write a short story with Jean. Again, I wondered if my deepest interest in her was as a writer I could take advantage of. I did not like this feeling. Though I wanted to start writing the story immediately, I let it drop; I wanted her to realize the idea came from her, not me, and it was up to her to act on it. But, too, I wanted to let her know I was interested; she very quickly imagined no one was interested at all.

She said, "What names shall we use for the old woman and the young man?"

"I'll get some paper," I said.

"Yes, do."

I visited Jean often, and each time we worked a little on the story. I wrote bits of it at home and read them out to her; she corrected. The manuscript became very messy. One of Jean's notes, dictated, was: "Cut down on her drink. Only two goes of malt whisky." Jean was responsible for most of the dialogue, I for the description. She gave the piece its name: "Shades of Pink". As, after a couple of weeks, I became more interested in finishing the story, Jean seemed to me to become less so. Finally she said, "You keep it now and do what you want with it. It's a gift." At home, I cut it down to a few pages, following the advice she said Ford had given her: 'When in doubt, cut." I put it in a bottom drawer.

Jean stayed on in the hotel over the winter. She was correcting the proofs of her collection of short stories, *Sleep It Off, Lady*. She once asked me to read out the story "Rapunzel, Rapunzel". She asked me to cut a sentence, then said, "It's a bad story. They're all bad stories. Mediocre. Worse than bad. What can I do? The reviews, quite rightly, will be condemning. I shouldn't have allowed them to be published. But it's done, they'll be published, and maybe it won't matter. What I wanted to do was to write my autobiography, but no one seems interested in that. I can't do it myself. No one can help me."

From her letters, I knew that Jean could write only with great difficulty, her words large and shaky. I had also seen her sign books for visitors, holding the pen clenched between her thumb and middle finger and jabbing it at the paper.

I said, "Look, Jean, if it's a question of your needing someone to write down what you want to dictate, I'd be happy to do that."

She looked at me; she appeared doubtful. "Would you?"

The uncomfortable feeling came over me. "Of course I would."

"You see," she said, "I just wanted to get down a few facts to correct the lies that have been said. I want to do that before I die."

We started, I think, the next day, after lunch. She sat in a chair with a big pillow behind her, and she had one drink to get her going. She dictated a passage which, in relation to her fiction, followed on directly from *Voyage in the Dark*; the heroine of that novel, who lived in Langham Street, might have written the opening sentences of Jean's dictation, recalling her recovery from her "illegal operation": "After I got better, I stayed on in the flat in Langham Street . . . I didn't see him, but he sent me a big rose plant in a pot and a very beautiful kitten."

After a few pages of dictation, she fell back on the cushion and closed her eyes; she suddenly opened them, shook her head, and said, "Never mind. Let's have a drink now."

We sat drinking, and she, lounging back on her pillow, told me stories from her life. We were very easy with one another, and in the easy way she talked about her life, I talked about mine. We were spirited. But it was when we talked about writing that we got excited. Her excitement was in her eyes.

She said, "I think and think for a sentence, and every sentence I think for is wrong, I know it. Then, all at once, the illuminating sentence comes to me. Everything clicks into place."

What had happened to us in the bathroom was not more

personal than our talk about writing; if we could talk about what had happened, we could talk about writing in the most open and vulnerable ways, which, perhaps, we would not want anyone else to hear.

I felt I could ask her anything. I said, "Do you ever think of the meaning of what you write?"

"No. No." She raised a hand. "You see, I'm a pen. I'm nothing but a pen."

"And do you imagine yourself in someone's hand?"

Tears came to her eyes. "Of course. Of course. It's only then that I know I'm writing well. It's only then that I know my writing is true. Not really true, not as fact. But true as writing. That's why I know the Bible is true. I know it's a translation of a translation of a translation, thousands of years old, but the writing is true, it *reads* true. Oh, to be able to write like that! But you can't do it. It's not up to you. You're picked up like a pen, and when you're used up you're thrown away, ruthlessly, and someone else is picked up. You can be sure of that: someone else will be picked up. No one in England has been picked up in a long while, no one in Europe, no one in America—"

"In South America?"

The expression burst from her like a revelation. "Yes! Yes!" Then she paused. "Perhaps."

I asked, "Do you ever wonder why one is picked up?"

"I don't know why," she said. "I don't know, and I wonder if it was right to allow oneself to be picked up. I wonder if it was right to give up so much of my life for writing. I don't think, after all, that my writing was worth it."

I said, "You couldn't help it, could you?"

"No. But it kept me so much to myself."

"Perhaps that's what you really wanted," I said.

"Yes, perhaps," she said. "I imagine you like to be alone a lot, don't you?"

"Yes," I said, "I do. I think there's more than a little monk in me."

"And there's a lot of nun in me," she said.

I went to see Jean week after week, three or four days a week. Sometimes she was too tired to dictate, having been out to lunch or to shop the day before. We talked. I half imagined she told me a lot about her life hoping I would write it all down; but I felt, whenever I did at home write down what she had told me that day, that I had been listening to Jean for the sake of writing down what she had said, and I wrote down, not what she said, but my reactions.

One grey day in late March, after she had dictated on previous visits a number of disconnected bits about her life, we tried to organize them chronologically. She found this very difficult, as she couldn't recall the sequence of events of so many years before. I had been careful not to interfere in what she dictated; I told her I was the one machine she could use. (She had never learned to type because she couldn't understand machines. She refused to speak into a tape recorder because it was an incomprehensible machine. It took me three visits to teach her how to open a compact she was given as a gift.) But now I began to help her to sort out the months and years of her life: 1917, 1918, 1919. She often passed her hand over her face in her attempts to remember, and when she slumped back on her pillow, as if, suddenly, uninterested, I said, "Come on, Jean, when did you and your husband stay at Knokke-sur-Mer and for how long?" She raised herself from the pillow and tried to concentrate. She said, "All I can remember is the sea, cold and green." "Try," I said. "1923, I think," she said, "and we stayed for two weeks. It was cheap. We bathed. We recovered."

I stayed with her a long time, till long past her supper. The more we got into the chronology, the more muddled Jean became, until, her hands to the sides of her head, she said, "I can't go on, I can't. This isn't the way I work." We never again attempted to make a chronology.

On my next visit, she had gifts for me: a shirt with red and blue flowers printed on it and a white pullover. She said, "Try them on." I went into her bedroom and put them on. When I came out, she studied me. "Go get one of my scarves," she said, "from my room, and tie it round your neck." I did. I came out. "Now walk around," she said. I walked around the small sitting room. "Look in the glass," she said. (She hated the word "mirror", as she hated the word "perfume"; she used "looking glass" and "scent".) I looked at myself. Jean was silent, as if silently judging. "Yes," she finally said, "very nice." I went to her and, laughing, put my arms around her.

By the time she was to leave London to return to Devon, I had covered thirty yellow and blue foolscap pages, back and front, with dictation. Sonia had typed them out.

I visited Jean briefly on her last day at the hotel. Sonia was packing for her. I kissed Jean goodbye. "Pray for me," she said. "I will," I said, "and you pray for me." "I will, honey," she said.

2

IN NOVEMBER, JEAN came back to London. She was put into a small flat in Chelsea, just across the Thames from where I lived in Battersea. She had a young woman to help her with her bath and dressing, and her friends to prepare lunch and dinner, and to entertain her. She didn't like the flat. The walls of the sitting room were green. Bad luck. She was quite sure it was a mistake to have come up to London, but she so hated Devon in the winter; maybe, though, she would return to her cottage when she recovered a little from her trip.

She had, over the summer, dictated more of her autobiography to a young writer who lived near her in Devon. This more consisted of memories of her early life on the West Indian island of Dominica, where she was born. It would make up the first part of the autobiography. She asked if I would continue to help her if she stayed in London. I was writing myself, but I said, "Yes, of course."

Often, crossing Chelsea Bridge on my way to her, I would think: You don't want to go to Jean's, you want to stay home to do your own writing. Also, I had very little money, and thought I should use the time I was with Jean to do a translation job, or write blurbs or book reports for a publisher.

Helping her became difficult. She needed a drink to start, a drink to continue, and yet another, and after two hours she was muddled, couldn't remember what she'd been saying, and she'd repeat, over and over, that, say, Victorian knife-sharpeners were terribly good, you just stuck the knife in and turned the handle and the knife came out sharp and clean, so you didn't have to clean it on wood, and the knives were much better than stainless steel ones—which showed that in many ways the Victorians were very clever, not what people think now. But people don't understand. No one understands. No one! I was never quite sure what she wanted to go into the autobiography and what, drunk, she was simply talking about. I put in everything I thought interesting, condensing it often to a sentence fragment to insert somewhere later: the Victorian knife-sharpener her father brought from England so the help wouldn't have to sharpen the knives on wood. A flash of anger would sometimes pass through her eyes when I'd read a passage to her to make sure I'd got it right, and she'd say, "No, that's not right."

In a little black briefcase that opened into a file, she kept the many bits and pieces of the autobiography, plus earlier writing on yellowing, torn paper. I wanted to go through these and sort them out, but I couldn't presume; they seemed in the file to be very private. The time came in our work, however, when we needed to organize the autobiographical pieces. Versions of the same section, or detached paragraphs, confused her; she would ask me to read the different versions, she would choose what she thought the best, and then tell me to tear up the others. I tore up wastepaper baskets full. She seemed to get satisfaction from this, as if getting rid of something was a great clarification. (And, in fact, she told me that to her writing was a way of getting rid of something, something unpleasant especially. She asked me once to write down for her a short poem that was going round and round in her head: "Two hells have I / Dark Devon and grey London— / One purgatory: the past—" And after I wrote it down she said, "Thank God, now I can forget that.") After as much clarification as could be made by tearing up, there still remained a mass of bits.

Jean often talked of the "shape" of her books: she imagined a shape, and everything that fit into the shape she put in, everything that didn't she left out, and she had left out a lot. She could not see the shape yet of the autobiography. Some chapters were together, some were in fragments, and she wasn't at all sure of the order of the chapters, much less the fragments in the chapters. We spent days trying, in our minds, to fit together pieces; Jean would often say, "It can't be done. It's too jumbled." To remember the pieces, we gave them names. I might say, "Well, Jean, this bit about your mother, don't you think it should go into the Mother chapter?"

One evening, as I was sitting with her while she ate her soup, I said, "Jean, why don't I do a paste-up of what's already been done of the autobiography?"

"A paste-up?"

I tried to explain, but it was like trying to explain a computer system to her.

She said, "If you think so."

"I'll do it tonight. You'll see, it'll help us."

She said, "Please put it all in chronological order and cut out all the repetitions."

I took the entire autobiography with me. Crossing Chelsea Bridge, the feeling came over me, as it often comes over me to jump when I am at a height, to throw the folder into the river. In my small study, before the gas fire, I spread pages and parts of pages on the floor. I cut out paragraphs which Jean had wanted to save from what she wanted to throw out. I cut in half a section called "The Zouaves". I pasted the pages and paragraphs and sometimes single sentences in what I thought the right order on to large sheets.

The next day I brought the paste-up to Jean and read the whole thing straight through. She said nothing. As I read, I saw her, her head tilted to the side, glance sideways from time to time at the page.

I asked, hoarsely, "What do you think?"

"Fine," she said weakly.

"Now," I said, "I'll take it home and type it all up."

I left when her editor came in to help her to bed.

In the morning her editor rang me. She said that Jean had got into a frightful state after I left, so frightful the editor hoped she would never have to see anyone in such a state again. She was drunk and swearing and thought I had destroyed her book; she thought, too, I would lose it. She was particularly upset that I had cut in half a section called "The Zouaves". She said, "It's David's book now, not mine." Her editor asked if we could have lunch the following day.

I spent all that day and the next morning typing out the paste-up. I put the two halves of "The Zouaves" together. Before

I went to lunch, I stopped by Jean's flat and left off the new typescript.

I said, "Jean, this is *your* book, not mine or anyone else's."

She said, "Of course it is, and if I don't like it I'll tear it up and throw it away."

"Good," I said.

I decided on my way to lunch that I would have nothing more to do with it. I thought Jean might have instructed her editor to say as much; but, in her office, she gave me a cheque for £500. Jean's editor said the cheque was from the publishing house; later, Sonia told me that in fact it came from Jean, who had instructed her editor to tell me it came from the publishers.

I did not mention the autobiography again to Jean. I saw her often, as it was the holiday season. On New Year's there was a champagne party in her flat. She, sitting in the midst, raised her glass and said, sadly, "Oh well, another year." She was wearing a long silver dress. Her friends were about her.

Shortly afterward, when I went to give Jean her evening soup, I found a close friend with her, in a haze of smoke. We all talked for a while, then the friend left. Jean asked me, timidly, if I could continue to help her. I was reassured, and thought: Well, I wasn't paid off. I wondered if she had been discussing it with the friend.

I said, "I'm very happy."

"Why?" she asked.

"Well, three reasons. My agent likes my new book."

Jean clapped her hands and laughed and said, "Hurrah."

"Then," I said, "I dropped a glass on the kitchen floor and it didn't break."

"Oh, that's great luck," she said.

"And because I'm here."

She said, "That's very tactful."

We sat with drinks, talking about writing in a very simplistic way.

I asked, "Have you ever thought about your readers?"

She shook her head. "No, never. They're sheep. Sweet. I appreciate them. But they're sheep, they follow after. And I never thought about money or fame. You mustn't ever think of money or fame. The voices go if you do. I don't think about anything but my writing."

"You don't think about yourself?"

She laughed. "I always thought I was different. I always thought I was a freak, that I felt things they didn't feel."

"Who?"

She shrugged. "They."

I laughed. "The ones who don't understand?"

"Yes, all of them. I've always felt best when I was alone, felt most real. People have always been shadows to me, and are so more and more. I'm not curious about other people—not about what they do, a little about what they think—and the more dependent I become on people, as I must, the more I shy away from them. But you like people, don't you?"

"Sometimes," I said, "yes, I do."

"And you're optimistic."

"In small ways."

"You are in person," she said, "but I don't know if you are in your writing."

I laughed.

"People don't like me," she said. "I know they always try to put me down. They think I'm not nice."

I said, "Sonia, who is totally honest, once said to me, 'Oh David, no one thinks you're as nice as you try to be.'"

Jean laughed; she liked that.

I asked, "Are you curious about yourself?"

"Yes," she said. "I shouldn't be. A mystic would say I shouldn't be. But I delve and delve. I don't know other people. I never have known other people. I have only ever written about myself."

"Yes," I said. "But doesn't that make you selfish?"

"Very," she said. "You have to be selfish to be a writer."

"Monstrously selfish?"

"Monstrously selfish," she said. "But you've also got to realize that if you're going to be that selfish you can't expect anything from anyone."

"And you're upset that you're so dependent now on others?"

She spoke in a flat, tired voice. "I'm a prisoner. I can't go out to shop, I can't prepare my own food, can't bathe alone, or make my bed. I worry that people resent my depending on them. And they do, of course they do."

"But do you in any way feel justified in accepting help because you're writing?"

She raised her hands and dropped them. "Oh, that: writing. No, nothing ever justifies what you have to do to write, to go on writing. But you do, you must, go on. You hear a voice that says, 'Write this,' and you must write it to stop the voice. I don't hear any voices any more. My last collection of stories was no good, no good, magazine stories. I wasted two and a half years on that book. Not good. Oh, the reviews say it's good. But you know when you've done something good, and those stories are no good. I can't do it any more."

She said it in such a sober, straight way I almost said, "Yes."

She said, "Let's have more drinks, honey. I know I'm not supposed to, but—the sins of the flesh and drink are very minor sins, aren't they?"

There was very little drink left. I had to run out to buy another bottle of gin and of sweet vermouth.

She was sitting in the middle of the couch. She said, when I sat on my chair, "David, what will I do with my life?"

"What would you like to do?"

"I want to go away, I want to do something really wild, really really wild. What shall I do? I'm a prisoner."

Her small body appeared to me more hunched and twisted than ever, and locked in that position, so when she moved even her head her entire body, rigid, moved too, in jerks.

"I once tried to commit suicide," she said, "a long time ago. I cut my wrists. The doctor when I got to him sewed me up as if he'd done it six times before that same evening. I thought he'd be angry with me, send me to an asylum, but he didn't say anything to me."

I said, "Jean, would you like to hear some music?"

"Yes," she said, "the Polovtsian Dances. I saw *Prince Igor* once in Nice."

I put the record on, just at the part I knew she liked; the music was filled with the crackling and popping of scratches. She raised her gaunt arms high as the music pounded, and seemed to be punching the air above her head with her fists, her head lifted to look up, tears pouring down her cheeks, and she said, "It's so alive! It's so marvellous!"

The moment the particular dance she liked ended, she lowered her arms, wiped her eyes with her hands, and said, "That's enough of that."

When I next went to work with her, I found her, on the divan, surrounded by cosmetics: compacts, lipsticks, creams. She was rubbing colours from a little flat box of many different shades of eye makeup on to the back of her hand. She was excited. "Look at this," she said, "someone sent me all this. It'll keep me happy for weeks." I asked her who had sent it all, but she couldn't remember. I sat next to her, and we discussed the shades of makeup that might best suit her. She took out her compact to look in the mirror and try a shade; I was worried that with her shaking hands she'd get it in her eyes. She smeared some on a temple. Looking at herself in the little round mirror, she raised her upper lip as in a sneer. She dropped her hand.

"You know," she said, "being attractive is alien to women, so when they try the strain shows."

I didn't know what she meant, and I didn't ask her.

She asked me, before we got to work on her autobiography, if I would help her with some correspondence. I got her to a chair by the desk and I opened a drawer to a heap of torn-open letters. She put on her spectacles, and reached out for a letter from the heap, examined it closely without, I thought, reading it, and handed it to me. Some letters were from acquaintances. We discussed whether she should answer them, but as all the letters said the sender would be in touch again, Jean asked me to tear them up. When we came across statements from publishers or letters from her accountant, she would put her hands over her eyes and say, "I can't, I can't." She never knew who her foreign publishers were or what, exactly, was happening to her books; and she never knew, no matter how often she was told, how much money she had, except, she was sure, that it was very little. Letters from fans she asked me to read out to her and as I did she looked wistfully sad. If the letters enclosed reviews, she asked the title and the first line, then said, "Tear it up." When the title was "The Dark Underworld of Women" or "The Woes of Women" or had "women" in it in any way, she'd grab the review from me and tear it up herself and throw it in the basket, laughing, and say, "No, I've had enough of *that*!"

It is impossible to say what Jean's attitude was towards any subject. She seemed to have little interest in reactions to her work from serious readers, and I think she found it improbable that any opinion of hers should be taken seriously in the world; and yet she raged that no one paid any attention to her, no one at all. I wrote down some of the things she said about women: "I'm not at all for women's lib. I don't dislike women exactly, but I don't trust them. You can never tell them what you really think, because if they know what you think they'll do you down. I'm not, I've never been intimate with them. It's not worth it. Sometimes I think I'm not like other women, that I lack feminine qualities. I'm not, and I have never been jealous, for example, never, and women are very jealous of one another." And: "Don't tell anyone this. Women are kind, but they do for you what *they* want to do, not what *you* want to do. They can't imagine that you may want something quite different from what they want. Men at least try to do for you what *you* want." And when women who were not close friends spoke to her, she looked at them with a superior and wounded tolerance as she listened, and said in response, simply, "Perhaps."

To have argued with Jean about her opinions would have been mad: she simply would not have understood if one had said, "But Jean, don't you wonder *why* you say that about women?" In terms of psychology (she said she had never read Adler, Jung or Freud, didn't know what they were about, and didn't want to know) or social studies (she wouldn't have understood what a social study was), she never asked why her main female characters acted as they did: they just did, as she did. There is about them a great dark space in which they do not ask themselves, removing themselves from themselves to see themselves in the world in which they live: Why do I suffer? When Jean said she delved and delved into herself, I didn't understand; it was certainly not to question her happiness, or, more, unhappiness, in terms of the world she lived in, and certainly not her prejudices. These prejudices were many, and sometimes odd: Protestants, Elizabethans—

When the time came for dictating, Jean said she wanted to do something unrelated to the book. I settled her on the divan with a drink. She began, "Today, I realize I am old, irretrievably old." I wrote. As she dictated, I became angry, and I kept asking myself: Why am I wasting my time with this? The long paragraph was banal and affected, and the more banal and affected it became the more she wept as she dictated. She said, "A sort of despair", in a sentence, and when I read the sentence to her, she said, "Cut the 'a sort of' and leave just 'despair'." She said no one helped her, she was utterly alone. She said she had had to come up to London on her own, when, in fact, Sonia and her editor had gone to Devon to stay in the village for three days to get her ready, and drove her up to London to the flat they had found for her. She asked me to read the whole thing out. She said, afterward, "Well, there are one or two good sentences in it." I wondered how much of the "incredible loneliness" of her life was literature, in which she hoped for one or two good sentences—all, she often said, that would remain of her writing, those one or two good sentences. I thought: She is false, and I am false for being here. I was annoyed, not because Jean was being unfair (one of her most commonly used expressions was "it's not fair!") but because she was being totally unimaginative; I expected more from her.

She said, when I gave her another drink, "Trust only yourself and your writing. You will write something marvellous if you trust yourself and don't give up." And though I clasped her free hand and squeezed it, I became more angry—with Jean, but mostly with myself. She went on, a little drunkenly, about writing. She said, "People think they can sit down and write novels. Nonsense. It isn't done that way. It's not a part-time occupation, it's your life." I resented what she said, thought everything she said was false, and didn't want to hear it; I sat across from her, drunk myself, and listened.

She put her glass down. "All right," she said, "I'm ready to do some work on the autobiography."

Quickly, and it seemed to me without thinking, she dictated this paragraph:

"Below the lonely house was the distant sea and Roseau Bay, and in the bay there was sometimes a strange ship flying the yellow flag, and we knew there was contagion on board. Rising up behind the house was untouched forest and, further up, a range of mountains, Morne Anglais, Morne Colle Anglais, Morne Bruce, Morne Diabletin. Morne Diabletin was the highest, and covered in mist. It had never been climbed because the summit was rock, and round the summit flew large black birds called devil birds. We could see the rain coming over the mountains and ran for shelter before it fell on us. There were a great many storms with forked lightning and thunder and great wind and heavy showers of rain, after which it cleared instantly, and the sky was blue again. When it was clear, the smell was fresh and sweet, and the sea below and the mountains above were bright."

I thought: This is beautiful, and it is because of this that I am working with her.

But the paragraph underwent many different changes. She kept saying, "It should be vague, more vaguely remembered." After a while, I was writing it with her, and she seemed to like the collaboration.

She said, after the paper and pencil were put away, 'You know, what I'm trying to write about, my life in Dominica, happened almost a century ago. I remember songs my great-aunt taught me which her mother had taught her. It all goes such a long way back." With another drink, she said, "And what is Dominica like now? They say there are no roses in Dominica now. There were, I remember them. They gave such a scent to the air." She suddenly shouted, "Lies! Lies!" She bared her teeth. "A pack of lies. And who cares? Who does anything? Terrible things people do. Getting rid of the roses in Dominica. I hate the word 'people'." She spat the word out. "People! I hate people! I hate everyone. I think they're all enemies. Terrible. No roses in Dominica. Who got rid of them? I know. I know. Up the Dreads. Yeah, the Dreads. They're in London, too, and they wear dark glasses. In Dominica they live in the forests. They're taking over. And who cares? Who gives a damn? Who? *No one* understands! Well, so what? I'll be dead soon."

I let her rage. Often she would open her compact, always with difficulty, and I'd watch her look in the little round mirror to powder her nose and cheeks and pull and push the hair around her face, her lips pursed with bitterness.

She suddenly stopped talking and looked at me for a moment in silence, blurry-eyed, then asked, "Why do you come to see me?"

I smiled.

She said, "I feel I can say anything to you, that you do understand, a little, just a little. Why do you come? Is it curiosity?"

I kept my smile. "A little."

"And what else?"

I didn't know what to say. I said, "For some mad reason, I love you."

"You're not pretending that?"

"I said it was mad. Could madness be a pretence?"

"No, it couldn't. I do trust you."

I thought: But why do I love her?

We didn't work the next time I saw her. One of Jean's close friends helped me to take her to a beauty clinic. She had been saying that no one understood how her morale depended on makeup and pretty clothes. She wanted her face done up and her lashes dyed black. The clinic was at the top of a very long flight of stairs, which we took one at a time, pausing at each step. In the rather severe grey waiting room, Jean said, "This looks serious." A young woman came for her, and I helped her up another flight of stairs into an alcove with green velvet curtains, then left to do shopping, and came back after an hour. She looked exactly as I had left her. In the car back to the flat, she said, "I am a fool." Then she giggled and said, "Well, I'll never go back *there* again."

I stayed with her for a few hours. We didn't work. She talked calmly about herself and, for the first time, about her family: her two older brothers, her elder sister, her younger sister. Her eldest brother, she said, studied medicine in Edinburgh, then went to India. The other brother, who had many illegitimate half-caste children in Dominica before he left (some still wrote to Jean and called her "dear Aunty"), went to Canada, then Australia, then East Africa, and finally died in England, "falling down a flight of stairs somewhere." Her elder sister, when young, went to stay with an aunt and uncle in the Bahamas, on a holiday, and stayed and stayed, until, Jean said, it was obvious she was not going to return to her own family. Then Jean herself, who left the West Indies when she was sixteen to study at a girls' school in Cambridge, was written to by her mother after her father's death and told there was no more money and that she should return; but Jean stayed in England and "sort of drifted away" from her family. Her younger sister came to England with her mother. Jean had hardly seen either of them. She wasn't in England when her mother died. Her sister, whom she never saw in later life, had died a few years before.

I said, "Do you consider yourself a West Indian?"

She shrugged. "It was such a long time ago when I left."

"So you don't think of yourself as a West Indian writer?"

Again, she shrugged, but said nothing.

"What about English? Do you consider yourself an English writer?"

"No! I'm not! I'm not! I'm not even English."

"What about a French writer?" I asked.

Again, she shrugged and said nothing.

"You have no desire to go back to Dominica?"

"Sometimes," she said, "but I know it will all have changed." She remembered something. "Honey, will you get from the top of the desk a piece of folded paper?"

I did, and gave it to her; she unfolded the paper to reveal three dried black leaves.

She said, "They're voodoo. Someone, I can't remember who, gave them to me. They're from Haiti. You put them under your pillow and you dream the solution to your problem. You can't drink too much and you can't take sleeping pills. I must try it tonight. I won't say I believe, and I won't say I don't believe."

She had the solution to her problem when I saw her again. She would do something really wild and go to Venice. Two close female friends would go with her. Jean asked me to come next time with two huge manila envelopes and a stick of sealing wax. We put the unfinished autobiography into the envelopes, sealed them with melted wax, and I wrote on each TO BE DESTROYED UNOPENED IF ANYTHING SHOULD HAPPEN TO ME, and she signed, with both Jean Rhys and E. G. Hamer. The envelopes were to be given to her accountant.

She said, "My work is ephemeral."

The work put aside, my following visits with Jean were chatty, and when I asked her about her life it was simply to get her to chat, and she did, with ease. I did not write anything down afterward in my diary, except this: "Jean told me she remembered seeing Sarah Bernhardt on the stage, in the last act of *La*

Dame aux camelias. It was after Bernhardt's leg had been ampu-
tated, and she did the whole thing on a chaise longue. Jean
recalled her saying, '*Je ne veux pas mourir, je ne veux pas mourir,*'
and a man in the seat next to Jean, tears streaming down his face,
said, 'But she's just an old woman with one leg.' Jean herself
began to weep; she took a handkerchief from her bag and wiped
her eyes and said, laughing, 'I'll bet my tears are ninety per cent
gin.' I felt close to her."

Sometimes we talked about writers, and she admitted, with no
sign of great regret, that she hadn't read Balzac, Proust, Fielding,
Trollope, George Eliot, James, Conrad, Joyce. She couldn't read
Austen, she had tried. She had read a lot of Dickens. She had read,
and remembered in great patches, the English Romantic poets,
and Shakespeare. Her favourite writer, she said, was Robert
Hichens, who wrote turn-of-the-century melodramas; she said
his books took her away, especially *The Garden of Allah*. But
when friends brought her his novels from second-hand book
shops she left them in a pile. She read, instead, thrillers, and in her
late life she read almost nothing else but. In Chelsea, she read,
over and over, a novel called *The Other Side of Midnight*, and she
said, "It's trash, perfect trash, but it takes you away," and made a
sign as of going away, far off, with her hand. She said it was very
important for a writer to have read a great deal at some time in his
life. I presumed this was when she was a girl in Dominica, when
she read books from her father's library and from the public
library, where she sat on a veranda to read, with a view of the sea.
While she was on tour in music hall the girls read *The Forest
Lovers*, and Jean read it too. It was about a couple in the Middle
Ages who ran away into the forest because everyone disapproved
of their love, but they always slept with a sword between them.
The sword, Jean said, was an endless topic of conversation.
("What a soppy idea. What'd they do that for? I wouldn't care
about an old sword, would you?") *The Forest Lovers* was the only
book Jean read for years. She must have read when she started to
write, though I am not sure what. She spoke very highly of
Hemingway, and she knew many modern writers at least well
enough to comment on them. About Beckett, she said, "I read a
book by him. It seemed to me too set up, too studied."

Shortly before she was to leave for Venice, amidst all the

organization, she developed a slight cold. She thought she shouldn't go. The doctor said she could. On my last visit before she left, she was wrapped in a quilt, and had a silk scarf tied as a turban around her head. Her cold, she said, was worse. She really thought she couldn't go to Venice. She said she'd been reading a guide book about the city which said it was full of rats. She looked at me as if she had found out something everyone had deliberately kept from her to give her a false impression, and she had now found out the truth for herself. I said, "But there are a lot of cats." She raised her eyebrows.

When I left her, telling myself I shouldn't, I fantasized that Jean would die in Venice, the typescript of the unfinished autobiography would be destroyed, and I would be left with the handwritten pages of dictation. I, alone, would have Jean Rhys's secrets.

This was in late February 1977. In November of the same year Jean returned to London for the last time. She stayed for months in the house of friends, where she had a bedroom and sitting room with pink floors. The friends helped her buy new dresses, and in her new dresses she sat in the sitting room off her bedroom and received visitors. But she would say, "I don't want to see anyone," and, ten minutes later, "No one ever comes to see me."

We resumed work on the autobiography. She had done very little on it over the summer and autumn, but she had made a mess of it. I sorted it out. Each time I came back it was messed up again. I would put it in order, with clips; she would ask to see it, the whole thing would fall apart in her lap and to the floor, and she would say, "I don't know if this will ever be finished, it's in such a mess." Finally, I put each section, or chapter, in a different coloured folder, wrote in big letters the names of the sections on the folders, and numbered them. If, however, there was more than one version of the section in the folder, she would become confused; I had to make sure there was only one copy, and the previous working copies I tore up and threw away in Jean's presence. This tearing up and throwing away satisfied her for a time.

The days were dark grey and rainy; we had to light the lamps shortly after lunch, when we began the work. I read, countless times, the sections she wanted to hear again, and at the end she always said, "That needs more work," but she never got around to doing the work unless I said, "All right, let's do it now." As often as I read certain passages to her, she always wept at some and laughed at others; she might have been hearing them for the first time. I thought: Yes, she's right, it will never be done. Many days, she couldn't work.

I began to take the separate sections home and I worked on them in my study; she knew this, and approved at least to the extent that, when I read them out to her on my next visit, she said, "That's all right." Very slowly, we finished chapters, and these were typed in triplicate. I threw away the working copy, put the top copy and the carbon in the folder, and gave Jean's editor the third copy, as I thought that now the work, however little there was of it, should be preserved. Sometimes she had me rework the top copy, and the corrections I transferred to the carbon, then threw the top copy away. When, at times, she asked where the top copy of a chapter was, I would try to explain what I had done, but she didn't understand, and she simply raised her hands. I was worried that she thought I was stealing from her.

One day, when she said she was too tired to work, we talked; but I was tired, too, and found it difficult to keep up the talk. I had now heard Jean's stories many times.

I yawned.

She said, "You're bored."

I felt she was testing me. "No," I said, "no."

She said, "Well, I'm going to tell you something I've never told anyone else. Do you promise you won't tell anyone? Promise me."

I crossed my heart.

"You'll think I've told it to you before, and I have, part of it, but not all. I told you, didn't I, how my third husband Max and I settled, having failed to settle in other places, in the cottage in Devon. I accepted it without seeing it, partly because Max wasn't well, and we would be peaceful there. There were four small rooms. It was scantily furnished, and at first I thought it was rather nice. There wasn't much in the sitting room except a desk and a good chair in front of the desk. There was a big bed and also a dressing table in the bedroom. By the time I put our armchairs in the sitting room, however, it began to look very crowded. I took a dislike to it then, and lived in the kitchen mostly. And after I discovered that the kitchen was haunted by spiders and mice, the feeling of peace left me. I was trying to write *Sargasso Sea* at the time, but I had been interrupted time after time, and in this cottage I quite gave up." Jean rubbed her forehead and looked down. "As usual, I took refuge in bottles of wine, and would get pretty drunk every night. Instead of getting better my husband got definitely worse. He kept falling, the way I keep falling now. At last the doctor insisted that he should go into hospital. I protested violently against this, but it was quite useless. Max died in hospital. I was left completely alone." Jean let her hand fall to her lap; she kept looking down. "Alone, when I had nearly finished a bottle of wine, I'd pin on all the medals Max had had, for he had been in the RAF in the First World War, go out of the door, and shout, 'Wings up! Wings up.' I think I must have been pretty nearly crazy at this time." After a pause, Jean shook her head and her body, as with a shiver. "Never mind about that," she said.

After another pause, she said, "One day there was a knock at the door. I opened it and there was a young man I didn't know. When I asked his name and if he wanted to see me, he said, 'Don't you remember me? I'm your friend.' Then I vaguely remembered that one evening, when I was tormented by a pack of little boys while I was shouting, 'Wings up,' he had chased them away. So I asked him in and offered him a drink. I am still completely puzzled as to why this young man came to see me. He told me that he worked in the road outside, and would I speak to him if I saw him? I said of course I would, and I did keep a lookout for him after that, but I never saw him."

It began to get dark in the room, and I turned on a lamp with a sheer pink scarf draped over it.

"After my husband died, I was determined to run away. It was winter, and a friend got me a room in a very nice house in, I think, Earls Court. He had chosen a large, rather pleasant room, and I had a moment of happiness when they brought me in tea and smiled. I remember looking out of the window as I poured the tea, and thinking that I had escaped. Unfortunately, the heating failed, and the whole place got icy cold. I stupidly went to take a shower. I pulled at the shower, but the water was completely icy.

The landlady ended by sending for the doctor. He said I had had a heart attack, and I was in St Mary Abbots Hospital for two weeks. After the hospital I went to a convalescent home for two weeks. Then I went to a nursing home in Exmouth for another two weeks. It was while I was there that I began to want to finish *Sargasso Sea*, and decided that the cottage was a quiet place where I might be able to go on with it. Sitting at the long table in the kitchen, I did manage to fill two exercise books, but when I stopped and reread what I had done, I discovered that I had written one short chapter, and then about six more versions of it. It wasn't the chapter that appalled me so much as the fact that every one of the versions was the same. I had merely written the same thing over and over again, not changing a word. After that I gave up. It seemed to me that it would be impossible ever to write again. I had no money; it would be quite useless for me to borrow money from my brother to go up to London. I had only a few books, which I knew almost by heart. I spent my time walking up and down the passage, afraid of the spiders and the mice, and all the people in the village. I think it was one of the worst times of my life.

"One day the clergyman of the village called on me. My brother had given me an introduction to this man's wife, whom he knew, but after I had been several months in the place, they hadn't taken the faintest notice of me. So I was rather astonished at his appearing, and still more astonished that I liked him very much. He didn't talk of religion at all. I had heard of this man. He was supposed to have thousands of books in his rectory. Someone also told me that he was a great scholar. After that first visit, he came back almost every week. He even began to knock in a special way, so that I would know who it was and open the door. I think that the reason I began to value his friendship so much was that he had never read any of my books and doubtless would have thought them ephemeral if he had. At last I told him about the fear that was surrounding me now and that it was getting worse all the time, that I had begun to hate human beings, that I had to force myself to go out at all. Week after week he came. He told me over and over that there was nothing to fear. Now this is what I never told you before, what I've never told anyone. He asked me one day if I would take Communion. I said

I didn't know if I believed. He said, 'You were baptized, weren't you?' I said yes. So the next time he came he came with Holy Communion, with the host, and I got down on my knees, stuck out my tongue, and he placed the host on it. And then, you know, I started to write, and I finished the novel. If there was any fairness in the world, I would have dedicated it to him, but of course I didn't." Jean was silent, her hands in her lap. She raised them and looked at me. She said, "Only writing is important. Only writing takes you out of yourself."

On our work days, there was no inspiration. Jean quickly became drunk. I became drunk with her. The work sessions degenerated into her shouting, "Lies! Lies!" And she would look at me, her face hard, and say, "You don't understand."

Once, angry, I said, "I do understand."

She immediately sat back, her face softened, and she said, softly, "I don't mean you."

I gathered, then, that when she said "you" she meant a very general "you": people.

When she said, "You know what you must do. Do you? You must know, and you *must* do it." I wasn't sure if she meant what I or what people must do. "You know what you must do in your writing," she said. I became reassured: she was going to say that I must in my writing save all civilization. But she stared keenly at me, expecting me to reply to her repeated, "Don't you know?" I smiled. She said, "You must tell the truth about them." She slammed her hand down on the arm of the chair. "You must tell the truth against their lies." My anger gave way to sudden sadness.

She saw the sadness in my eyes. She said, "When I was a little girl I was always saying, 'That's not fair, that's not fair,' and I was known as socialist Gwen. I was on the side of the Negroes, the workers. Now I say, 'It's not fair, it's not fair,' about the other side, because I think they *aren't* treated fairly."

I simply looked at her.

Her face, it seemed to me, became that of a little girl. She looked at the floor. She said, "I don't know. I don't know any more."

Sometimes, in my reading, she would ask me to cut a passage I thought good. Often, I convinced her to keep it in, though she said it should be cut because she didn't understand it. One passage she wanted to cut, which I said really should stay in, was that as a child she imagined God was a big book. But a passage about her mother, which she said she simply could not understand, she insisted on leaving in:

She would often stick up for what she called their rights. We had a large mango tree which took up most of the room in the small garden. The fruit was round, small and very sweet. But the branches hung over the wall in such a way that when it bore fruit anyone in the street could get it. My father was furious as he liked mangoes and he couldn't bear to think that little boys stole them. He sometimes threatened to put broken glass along the top of the wall or buy another, fiercer dog. "Scap's no good," he'd say. My mother said, "You can't stop them from picking fruit if they are thirsty, they have a right to." "What right?" my father said; "those are my mangoes." "They have a right to it," was all my mother would say. She often talked like this about their rights, as she maintained that though all babies were sweet, black babies were much prettier. There still remained, however, this wide, cold gulf between her and them which she made no attempt to cross. She was a contradictory woman and as I grew older I stopped wondering what she thought and why.

And she insisted on cutting this, which she said was irrelevant:

There were two breezes, the sea breeze and the land breeze. People said that they called the land breeze the undertaker breeze. But I never thought that. It smelt of flowers.

She often had me check to make sure a passage she thought of using in her autobiography hadn't already been used in one of her novels or short stories. I did my best, but I, too, couldn't always remember.

When I arrived at the house and before I left, I sat with the friend with whom Jean was staying, and we talked, obsessively, about Jean.

I found the friend in tears once, sitting at the kitchen table. She said, "I feel I'm becoming like her. Yesterday she said to me, 'It's eight o'clock, thank God, now I can go to bed,' and at nine o'clock I was saying to myself, 'Thank God, now I can go to bed.'"

I said, "I guess I'd better go up to her. How is she?"

"She fell in the bathroom last night, getting up to pee. It was a struggle. I had to roll her on to a blanket and drag her back to her bed. But she's all right now."

Jean was in the bathroom when I got to her sitting room. I waited for her. She came out, unsteadily. She was wearing large pink bloomers, tied at the ankles, a white silk blouse, and her pink wig, put on backwards. She smiled when she saw me. I went to her, kissed her. She stood holding the back of a chair, and she appeared thoughtful.

"You know," she said, "I was just thinking about the differences in our writing. I can't make things up, I can't invent. I have no imagination. I can't invent character. I don't think I know what character is. I just write about what happened. Not that my books are entirely my life—but almost. You invent, don't you?"

I said, "I suppose I do."

I helped her to her chair across the room.

On the slow way, she said, "Though I guess the invention is in the writing. But then there are two ways of writing. One way is to try to write in an extraordinary way, the other in an ordinary way. Do you think it's possible to write in both ways?"

"No," I said.

"You understand?"

"I think so."

"I think what one should do is write in an ordinary way and make the writing seem extraordinary. One should write, too, about what is ordinary, and see the extraordinary behind it."

"Yes."

She dropped down among the bright pillows of her chair. "I have never, never got what I felt and thought into words."

"You think not?"

"No."

"And yet, when you dictate a sentence to me, I study it and think, this sentence should be banal and sentimental, and it's in fact original and tough. Why is that?"

"*Je n'sais pas*," she said.

Jean

"And there's a sense of space around your words."

"Yes," she said, "I tried to get that. I thought very hard of each word in itself."

I said, "Sometimes I think your writing is not only about your life, it is your life. I mean, you've had a few very intense experiences in your life, all isolated by great space and silence. Your words are like that, intense events which occur in space and silence."

"My life has been turbulent and very boring," she said.

I didn't want to start working. The best of Jean was not, now, in her writing, but her talk about writing. With one drink, however, she started, "Lies! Lies!" and when we tried to work her dictation was incoherent. I took down sentences, sometimes words, to compose at home scrappy paragraphs. We were meant to be working on her later life. I was determined to finish at least a first draft. The deeper she got into her later life, the more incoherent she became. After half an hour, she couldn't work.

I told her about a dream I had had about a woman at a market stall from whom I, hungry, asked for a bun, and she said, "They're very expensive," but I said, "It doesn't matter," and as I was reaching into my pocket for the money she gave me the bun and money from her own pocket, and I suddenly understood that in the country I was in when you bought something you were in fact paid to take it.

Jean laughed. She said, "Dreams mean the opposite of what they say. That woman was me. You think I'm giving you something in the dream, but, deep down, you feel I'm taking something from you."

The autobiography was coming together in a rough way. The first part, which dealt with her life in Dominica, was at least in a completed draft. The second part, her life in England and France, had big holes.

In the black file which Jean had with her were yellow scraps of earlier stories; we went through them, and some of these, because they were her life, we transferred to the second part of the autobiography. Among the scraps was an old brown-covered notebook, half the pages torn out. Jean took it out.

"I don't know," she said, "if this should go in. I wrote it, a kind of diary, a long time ago, when I was living in a room above a pub called the Ropemaker's Arms in Maidstone."

"Why were you living in a room above a pub in Maidstone?"

She made a face. "Max was in Maidstone prison. I have always been attracted, I suppose, to thieves and saints, not that they were thieves exactly, and they weren't saints. I didn't know, and I don't know now, why my first and third husbands were sent to prison. I don't know much about my husbands, and I don't know much about my parents. Perhaps I wasn't curious. My daughter once told me my first husband, Jean, was in the French Intelligence. I didn't know. Max was married before, but whether he had any children or not I don't know—perhaps a boy or girl. Men used to come to the house. I didn't like them, especially one. I didn't know what Max did with them. He went to prison. Enough. I've enough letters with the heading HM PRISON. I visited him. One prisoner said to me, 'It's all right for people like me, we should be here, but not for people like him.' The warder with the one leg was nice. Max got a bit of money in prison and he saved it to buy me chocolates. The whole thing was so beastly I try not to think about it. I know the real villain, that one man I especially couldn't stand, went free. Max never recovered." She held the notebook out to me. "Anyway, I wrote this in my room. I called it 'Death Before the Fact'. Do you know that? It's from St Theresa. In my room were two black elephants with long curving tusks on the mantel, and from the window I saw laundry and cabbage stumps. Will you read it to me? You'll see how long ago I wrote it, because the handwriting is clear."

I read. Jean had put herself on trial. She saw herself, defenseless, answering the questions of a judge who condemned her to a simple fate: to be unhappy, to write, and to die.

She asked me if I would take the notebook home and type it out. I did.

On the margins of the pages torn out were words, and these I typed out too, though I decided I would not tell her I had done so.

My dear . . . I've just . . . worrying . . . to help . . . a little . . . to me . . . know . . . Leslie . . . called . . . Edward . . . with . . . why they . . . took such . . . will be free . . . We are supposed . . . London . . . money . . . that I . . . lives . . . for a little . . . I can't . . . them . . . me . . . all . . . I didn't want . . .

went . . . because . . . down . . . Hell . . . I do . . . place . . .
the . . . tell . . . was . . . just before Max . . . approached by
. . . a radio play . . . and I would . . . from . . . I can't . . . well
. . . going . . . here . . . person . . . But I fear . . . hopeless . . .
do so . . . looking . . . live . . . My Dear Edward . . . The
enclosed . . . Will you . . . I have . . . you please . . . is likely
. . . careful . . . but . . . I . . . you . . . allowance . . . I gave
. . . worried . . . living . . . where . . . I get 36/6 a . . .
Admiralty . . . from the P . . . from . . . that is . . . but . . . for
the . . . 30/ . . . as . . . by . . . I . . . by . . . out . . . So I'm
going to . . . I married . . . know because . . . Brenda . . . to
be . . . to get . . . it . . . died I . . . sincerely wish I . . . So I'll
. . . oh how I wish . . . of waiting . . . I . . . been . . . stresses
. . . to see . . . and leave . . . approve of them . . . safeguards
. . . that my . . . only be . . . think . . . I'm afraid the . . . gone
on . . . I . . . after . . . kind things . . . so badly . . . to feel . . .
else . . . has . . . dread . . . year . . . looking . . . be fair . . .
you'd paid . . . lasted . . . friendly . . . after hearing . . . still
. . . Strauss . . . As for the other . . . home that . . . a looney-
bin . . . that at all . . . Brenda and . . . you must . . . necessary
. . . You . . . who . . . I . . . myself . . . do . . . myself . . .
after . . . A . . . only . . . he . . . them . . . Did you, either of
you . . .

When I came back and read the typed-out diary to her, she
thought she wouldn't include it in the autobiography. I insisted
she must. She said, "All right, if you cut certain passages." I cut
them, but include here only this:

Do you wish to write about what has been happening to you?
No, not yet.
You realize that you must?
I doubt whether it is as important as all that. Still I will write it,
but not today.
Softly, softly, cathee monkey.

I asked, guiltily, I suppose, as I had not only written about her
in my diary, I had now stolen from her, "Do you mind people
writing about you?"

"Yes," she said. "And I know people will try to uncover
everything about me after I die to write it all down."

"Well," I said, "you won't know."
"Perhaps," she said.

The February days continued the January days of dark grey. Jean was not well. She didn't know what to do. Perhaps she should return to her cottage in Devon where a nurse would take care of her, as she was utterly incapable of taking care of herself. The second part of the autobiography was still scrappy towards the end. I promised I would go down to Devon in the spring to help her; she smiled at me as she might smile distantly on all promises.

On my last visit, Jean was in bed. She had a plaster on her forehead covering a bruise she'd got from falling. She looked frail.

She said, "I want to tell you about an experience I had once." It was as if she had been thinking of it for a long time and had finally decided to tell me.

I asked, "Do you want me to write it down?"

"No," she said.

She said, "I've tried to write it, but have never been able to. It shows how inadequate words are. In Paris, some close friends suggested and paid for a holiday for me in the South of France. I went with another girl. This was in the Thirties. We went to Théoule, near Cannes. One day, alone, I had a bathe in the sea, then lunch. As I knew the bus to Cannes, where I wanted to go to shop, was leaving soon, I ate my lunch quickly, and I didn't have any wine. But I missed the bus, and thought, oh well, I'll walk, it isn't a long way. At La Napoule I felt tired and left the road to sit by the sea. You could do that in those days. I can't describe what happened. No words, no words, there are no words for it, except perhaps, in a still unknown language. I felt a *certainty* of joy, and terrific, terrific happiness, not only for me, but for everyone. I knew that the end would be joy. I felt, too, a part of the sea, the sun, the wind. I don't know how long I was there, but after a while I got up, went back to the coast road, and walked to Cannes. I went to a café for coffee. There was a big tree outside the café. I sat and I looked about and I thought: Why do I hate people? They're not hateful. When I got back to Théoule I of course said nothing to my friend, but my happiness for everyone lasted, lasted, perhaps three or four days."

I picked up my pencil and paper.

"Are you going to write it down?" she asked.

"Only if you want me to," I said.

"If you want to," she said, and she repeated it again as I wrote. Afterward, she looked out of the dark window on which rain was falling, and said, "Is there anything else I have to tell you? No, I don't think so. Anyway, none of the rest matters."

I stared at her.

She said, suddenly, "David, I think you've just seen my ghost."

I asked, "Do you believe in a life after death?"

She smiled. "Well, how can one be sure unless one has died? But I think there must be something after. You see, we have such longings, such great longings, they can't be for nothing."

"But you don't have any definite faith?"

"Oh, whatever faith I have I find expressed in man-made things, and to me the greatest expressions of faith I've ever seen are Botticelli's *The Birth of Venus*, and the Winged Victory of Samothrace."

"Do you see your books as an expression of faith?"

"My books aren't important," she said. "Writing is. But my books aren't."

Before I left, she said, "Give me the file, will you, honey?"

I put it on the bed beside her and with her spectacles she looked through the few scraps of old paper left in it. She took out a sheet.

"This is what I want to give you," she said and handed me the sheet. "It's the outline of a novel I wanted to write called *Wedding in the Carib Quarter*. I won't write it. Maybe you will."

I asked, "Will you sign it?"

She wrote on it, in large shaky letters that looked like Arabic script: "Think about it. It is very important." She gave it to me.

She said, "Someone once told me that. I won't tell you who."

3

I WENT TO Devon in May to see her. I didn't stay in Jean's garden shed, but with her only close friend, a retired teacher, in the next village. The teacher's great heroes were Karl Marx and Groucho

Marx; in the past she had had arguments with Jean about politics. She said Jean was not liked in the village because, years before, she had told some little boys she would cut them into pieces, which gave her the reputation of being a witch. "But she's suffering now from senile persecution. We can't judge Jean from the way she's been these past years. It'd be like judging the whole of Hardy's life from his last years."

In rain, I went to Jean's cottage before noon. The cottage, behind a high hedge, had been constructed during the war for evacuees. Jean came slowly to the door. As I kissed her, she said, "I should have rung you to tell you not to come." I said, "It doesn't matter if we don't work on the book. It's lovely to see you." "Oh, me!" she said. Then she looked down at the passage floor.

We sat in her little lounge.

She said, "It's all gone wrong, the whole country. Rain, rain, weeping for England. How I hate this country. How I hate this cottage."

I always wondered when she spoke like this if I should agree with her, if what she wanted from me was to agree with her; and I wondered, too, if I should try to cheer her up, if that's what she wanted.

I said, "But it's a pretty cottage."

"Yes, yes," she said, "pretty, but I want out, I want out, I want to take a pill and die." She dropped her head against the back of the chair, her mouth open, her eyes staring, as if she suddenly had died; then she shook her head, looked about the room, and said, "Where is our lunch?"

Her nurse prepared Jean's favourite lunch, curry and rice, which we ate at a little kitchen table. We drank very little.

Back in the lounge, Jean in a chair and I on a stool by her, I started to read straight through the autobiography, a lot of which I had memorized from so many readings.

"'Smile, please,' the man said, 'not quite so serious.'"

Jean stopped me. She said, "Now tell me honestly, David. Is this worth doing? I don't think it is. It's no good. It's dull. It has no life in it. And even if it did, what does it matter? Who cares?"

I said, "Jean, *you* told me writing is very important, and I tell myself that when *I* think, What does it matter?"

"I never understand you and your writing," she said. "I mean, I cannot imagine your writing coming from you. You're so, well, outgoing, and your writing is so, well, inward."

I didn't ask her to explain. I said, "Come on, let's do some work."

She looked at the floor for a while, then said, "Read me a little."

I read. She asked me to cut words, sentences, paragraphs. She sighed often and quickly became tired; her head sank more and more. I left before it was dark.

The following day she couldn't work. She raged, and in her rages she shouted, "It means nothing, it means nothing, writing, nothing, nothing!"

I stayed only a short time.

The retired schoolteacher said, "Go back to London. You really can't do much for Jean now."

I had been asked by a friend of Jean's in London, who had bought and had reupholstered in yellow a chaise longue Jean had specially wanted for her sitting room, to get a cheque from Jean to pay for it; when the next day I did ask Jean for this, she shouted, "I have no money! I have none! They all want to take money from me!" I suddenly thought: She may think I have come for money. I helped her make out the cheque, worried that she might later forget what it had been for, and accuse me of asking for it for myself. I sensed, while I was with her, the small trust she had had in me turn to suspicion; and I imagined I began to act suspiciously in trying to act large-spirited.

Without drink, Jean raged. Who cared about writing? Who? And why should anyone care, because it didn't matter.

I sat by her and said nothing.

She said, "David, you're young. You have your life ahead of you. Don't listen to what I say. Don't listen to me, I'll depress you."

That afternoon I left her to return to London. I had an hour in Exeter before my train and I went to the cathedral. I sat in a chapel. I felt very low. I knew that in my outer bright believing heart I had been false to Jean, because in my inner dark unbelieving heart I had loved her as a writer. I thought, But she might forgive me my cheap literary curiosity, she might even condone it; she might, perhaps, tell me that my literary interest, not only in her but in the world, was the deepest possible interest. And then it came to me that Jean was dead, because she was dead as a writer.

A year after Jean's death in 1979, I was at a table in a little glassed-in room in the Special Collections Department in the Library of the University of Tulsa, Oklahoma, looking through a selection of her papers. She had sold them to the Library—what little she had left, as she once told me she'd thrown out piles of manuscripts and typescripts—and I looked to find what I hadn't seen before.

In a large grey file box I found two notebooks. They were torn and smudged and covered with cigarette burns. The handwriting was round, looped, large—her early writing.

One notebook had on its back cover a stamp: *Cartoleria Pistoj, Firenze*. I wondered if Jean had ever been to Florence and bought it there.

I read:

> you know its awful bad I just live for the time when I can have a drink & cheer myself up a bit
> there's lots to that
> Well he said to me like that get out he said Get out where I said—I don't care where he said but get out
> Go on the friend said—her eyes were wandering
> I looked at him I said If I was to tell you what I think of you I would blow you out of the window I said You can go to hell I said.
> You cant go somewhere when you're there already I said

There was no punctuation. It wasn't clear who was talking. Was this, I wondered, a bit of diary or note-taking for fiction?

The second student's notebook had a map of Britain on the inside cover. At one end were pages written in her earlier handwriting, and, the notebook turned upside down and over, at the other end were pages written in her later, feeble hand. Between the two were blank pages.

I found many bits of poems, ballads, patois from Dominica. And in both notebooks I found, over and over, the first line of

what she had hoped would be her autobiography. "Smile please
the man said not quite so serious."

Then I read this, which I do not believe she used in any of her
fiction:

This vision came when I was walking along in the hot sun
thinking then not thinking & being intensely happy for I
existed no longer. but still the trees & the soft wind that smells
of flowers & the sea & I was the wind the trees the sea the warm
earth & I left behind a prison a horrible dream of prison & my
happiness impossible to write of it active laughing with joy—
Do you see now oh then it was just a dream of prison
& got to La Napoule
Yes of course what a fool I was worrying like that the certainty
I don't know how long this state of bliss
lasted then suddenly I was back in myself but the happiness was
not quite gone & I walked into Cannes had a coffee at that café
caught the bus back still happier than ever in my life though
just the shadow the remembrance of the other happiness

This happened walking along the road from Théoule to
Cannes one hot day in August about two to three o'clock I was
quite well & I had had no wine at lunch as I was late for the bus
to Cannes & hurrying up and I think I caught the one o'clock
bus

. . . Only through books sometimes I can get it

Sonia

ON THE EVENING I was rung up by Jean's editor and told that Jean had died in hospital in Exeter, Sonia Orwell came to dinner. When she arrived, I said, "It'll be a sad evening," because I imagined Sonia, who was perhaps closer to Jean than anyone else, would have been the first to hear. But she hadn't heard, and, in the passage where we stood, she stared at me for a long while. "May I use your telephone?" she asked. She rang different people; she wanted to find out what had happened and what she could do, and there was a dry gravity in her voice.

I went with Sonia and other friends by train to Exeter for the cremation. There were few of us in the chapel. Four men in badly fitting dark suits brought in a tiny white casket, placed it on a platform, and stood back; a minister read a passage from the Bible about "death in life", and a curtain closed about the casket.

Later, in a working men's pub by the train station, we all talked. Sonia said, "We didn't know what a rare bird had made its nest in our tree."

On the train back to London, everything I looked at was stark. Whenever I looked at Sonia, her face in the grey light appeared set; her narrowed eyes were hard.

Sonia, from Paris, wrote me a letter about Jean:

She was, towards the end, so very old and so senile so much of the time. And I think that people who live so much alone tend to 'highlight' just a few incidents or thoughts in their lives and come out with these over and over again while other things, since they've not been used to talking about them, never, never get mentioned—they've been buried too deep to dig up again. Jean was the sort of essence of someone who'd forgotten how to talk naturally through having been isolated, which accounts for the yards of subconscious she dragged up when drunk, her endless thoughts about the "unfairness of it all", blacks, politics, etc., because this is the way a lonely person behaves when she finds herself at last in company. I mean a person who wasn't really born to be solitary, rather the opposite, but finds herself alone through quirks of fate or character. I felt sad that you'd never known her as early as I did because there's no describing her charm, at moments, in those days, and also no describing how selfless she could be when she thought about her friends or other people or, indeed, people in general. I remember that winter when we moved her from that ghastly hotel to the one off the Portobello Road, I knew she was ageing so rapidly and I think being in that 'old people's' hotel must have been quite abominable to her. I remember her saying how awful it was to be old etc., but always adding, "But darling I'm not old *inside*" and how all that winter I heard distinguished aged people say exactly, but exactly the same thing in the same words: "I don't *feel* old inside", "I don't *feel* old *inside*." It was awful.

I think perhaps, too, you don't, or didn't quite realize that Jean did have reservations about you taking down her book just simply because you were a writer yourself. She told me time and time again how impossible it was for one writer not to, quite unconsciously, alter or rewrite another writer and I think she was torn between her quite clear understanding that you could perhaps help her more because you were a writer—after all what's a perfectly ordinary dim-witted young 'secretary' to make of a jumble of words which would have some magic for anyone who was of the *métier*—and her terror that two writers never have the same 'voice' and that, without meaning to, you were in fact writing her book for her in a way she wouldn't have written it herself. I do absolutely see her dilemma and in a sense she couldn't cope with it because she was too old, too helpless, and not lucid enough. But I think this explains why she wanted to talk about *writing* so much with you, and why she both so enjoyed doing this and again, perhaps you don't realize her generosity in this, why she wanted in any tiny way she could to help you. It also explains how hard it was for you to get her to do any long stint of work. Her terror of *you* writing *her* book would overcome her and drink would muddy up her mind entirely because she was drinking in a panic-stricken way. Yet she always wanted to *give* you something: an idea, a new shirt, some knowledge she just might have that you didn't. It was all much, much sadder than I think you realize.

I'm only so very glad she's dead. The other day I was walking along the street and suddenly saw *the* white choker which Jean had been wanting, and which we had been hunting for, for years, and I was overcome by a sort of relieved indifference: "It doesn't matter a damn that it's there," I said to myself and was amazed that I felt no grief: in fact felt nothing more than a sort of: "*Tiens*, pity it wasn't there some years ago," and *no* more.

Sonia had introduced me to Jean at a luncheon party at her house. At the head of the table of six people, Sonia talked while Jean, a little lady wearing a new spring hat and slumped in her chair, was silent; as Sonia talked, I noted tears rolling down Jean's face, but she didn't wipe them away and let them drip, she told me later, because she didn't want to draw attention to them and make a fuss. If Sonia noticed, she ignored Jean's tears; she kept the conversation general, and the general conversation was high over Jean's hat.

There was this strong sense in Sonia's treatment of Jean: that she would help Jean in whatever way she possibly could, even to washing and ironing her clothes, but Jean must not presume she was the only person in the world who was in a position to need help.

The next year, I was with Sonia in Jean's hotel room as Sonia made out a shopping list for a party. Jean said, "Please don't forget the vermouth for me." Sonia, baring her teeth, answered her, "Do you think you're the only person at the party who is going to drink?" Jean frowned and her eyes went vague. Sonia said, "Think first of what the people who are buying you the vermouth may want." Jean said quietly, "Yes."

Sonia seemed to think that Jean should feel no guilt for being helpless—helpless not only physically, but, by some accident of character, psychologically—but that she should feel guilty whenever she presumed on her helplessness as a means of making others attentive to her.

Sonia did not like people to talk about themselves in a group; alone with her, one could talk at great length about, not oneself, but one's problems with one's husband, wife, lover, friends, taxes, flat. Sometimes when I arrived at Jean's hotel I would find Sonia on the edge of a chair, leaning towards Jean, half reclining on a sofa among pillows, and I'd feel I had come into a room, filled with smoke, in which great intimacies had been exposed. Sonia would smile at me, and Jean, too, as from a far distance; I was sure Jean had been telling something to Sonia which she had perhaps not told anyone else, ever, and the revelation hung in the air like the smoke. If Sonia wouldn't let Jean think she was unique, Sonia herself thought she was.

While Jean was in London on her winter visits, I, when alone with Sonia, talked about Jean, and if I said, with a certain possessiveness, "Did you know that Jean was once. . . ?", Sonia always answered, "Of course I knew." Then she said, "I don't like your imagining you'll find out from Jean secrets which she wouldn't share with anyone else. Everything you've said about Jean that she's told you I've known, in greater detail, from her, and there is a great deal she has told me which she hasn't mentioned to you, I'm sure." "I'm sure," I said.

Then Sonia said to me, "I'm a snob. I'm not helping Jean because she's just anyone. I'm helping her because she's Jean Rhys."

In her world of special people—writers, painters, musicians, philosophers—Sonia thought of herself as someone to help them; and, among them, she would say, "Don't think you're special."

About Sonia, Jean said to me, "She is the only woman I trust."

Sonia organized Jean's London life for her, and exhausted herself doing it. She kept Jean's agenda—a sheet of paper ruled into large squares which Jean could see—filled. It was not easy to find people to visit Jean, and, often, they did not return for a second visit. If Sonia could not get anyone to visit, she went to Jean herself, at lunch time and supper time, and then put Jean to bed.

Sonia once came to dinner after having got Jean into bed with her hot-water bottle, her glass of milk and pills by her side, and having switched off her light, and Sonia said to me, shaking her head, "She's a monster. She's a total monster of selfishness."

At tea at Sonia's house, a friend, an actor who had made a date to visit Jean that evening, said, jokingly, that he was rather dreading the visit, and Sonia, staring hard at him, said angrily, "You don't understand at all how utterly, utterly lonely she is. You joke, and should be weeping, because Jean's state is desperate." He got up quickly and left for Jean's hotel. Sonia said to me, "No one, no one understands Jean's total, total desperation."

I thought that for Sonia to prepare breakfast for herself must have been almost beyond her because of exhaustion; with how much greater effort did she prepare parties for Jean, after which, she said, she would have to collapse completely.

Helping Jean, Sonia couldn't collapse, no matter how great the strain, because Jean needed her help.

One of the winters when Jean was in London, I took Germaine Greer along to her hotel to introduce them. Before we went in to see her, Germaine bought a bottle of champagne, and she and I followed a young man with the bottle into the room. Jean, sitting at the end of a sofa in her long blue, padded housecoat, jerked to attention, a look of bewilderment in her large eyes, the colour of her housecoat. At the other end of the sofa was another, younger woman writer.

Germaine sat in an armchair. As we drank champagne, she talked about breast cancer, and described how the breast is clamped into a kind of vise for the operation. Jean seemed to be listening closely, then she leaned towards the other woman and said that she had been to a shop and seen some pretty hats.

When, the next time I was with Jean, I asked her what she had thought of Germaine, she said, with that small jerk of her body with which she always started to speak, "I liked her. I'm sure she must be very courageous."

Germaine went down to Devon to visit Jean in her cottage.

At a drinks party, while I was speaking with Sonia, I saw Germaine stride towards us. She said to me, "I've solved the problem of how to help Jean." She and Sonia did not know one another; I didn't introduce them, as Sonia turned to Germaine, smiling with her teeth, and said, "We're perfectly capable of taking care of Jean ourselves, thank you." Germaine stepped back and turned away.

I

I WAS FIRST introduced to Sonia in Paris at the opening of an exhibition of paintings by a friend of hers. She wore a fur hat, and all the while she spoke to me, so rapidly I hardly understood her, she shoved her hat about her head. I hadn't got her name, and had no idea who was speaking to me.

She seemed to be making rapid comments on a great many subjects: England, France, America.

She didn't ask me any questions about myself, and I couldn't ask her any about herself.

During brief pauses, she looked at me, and I thought she might suddenly walk away, then she continued to talk, that furious talk, which had nothing to do with her or me, but which seemed to be addressed to people standing about us, whom she also looked at starkly. She repeated herself a lot; whatever the subject was, she, I thought at one pause, had exhausted it, and I tried to think of something to say, but she went on, repeating herself over and over. Perhaps she remained with me because she didn't want to leave me by myself in the crowded gallery, and she was repeating herself for lack of anything else to say. I hoped someone would come along and relieve her; but when someone did join us, instead of going off to others, Sonia stayed with us, and, shoving her hat so it almost tipped from her head, went on talking. After every brief pause, she said, as if she had heard someone contradicting her, "No, it is absolutely true that in England . . . in France . . . in America."

Then, after a stark look at me, she said, "No, as George used to say. . . ," and, with the authority of this George, whom I didn't know, she made a comment, and, her hands lifting her hat up and pulling it straight down so the fur was low over her forehead, her hard look seemed to soften as if she had, finally, stated her justification for all her chatter, and her look said, "You do know who George is, don't you?" All I knew was that he gave her authority.

I nodded.

She went on talking.

At the centre of the gallery, the painter and some of his friends, drunk, were tearing open telegrams and dropping them to the parquet floor, and laughing.

d to me that Sonia was also drunk.

ter, I was told her name, and realized who George
to recall her chatter, but I couldn't.

fter the opening, I went with the painter and a party
ary people, including Sonia, to lunch in a restaurant.
g a cap with a narrow peak, and, on the way into the
efore I could take it off, Sonia did; she kept it, and at
it on, then passed it to others, who put it on, until it
me.

talking furiously. It might have been about the hat. I
what it was about. She spoke in French. She pulled
rranged it, and, to arrange it again, ran her fingers
shook her head. Her hair was light, and she was, of
beautiful. She spoke French as if it were her own
d she spoke it in a loud voice. She often mentioned
here was more, much more, than kepis in her talk.
tles of wine were put on the table. Quickly drunk
ed that Sonia was drunk as quickly. She was never
ed to be looking at and listening to everyone at the
er anyone could talk. She would say, "*Non, non,
'est pas ça du tout*," and, disarranging or arranging
say what it was.

Frenchmen in the party, and when one spoke in
abruptly said to him, in French, "The French
speak any language they want, it doesn't matter
ause only French counts. It may be true that only
but knowing French is no excuse to speak other
. You shouldn't try to speak English, because
it. Really, people who try to speak languages
w—" She emphasized this by jerking her head
back, then forward, and saying, "Do you see?"

"Yes, Sonia, I see," he said.

I thought: Everyone is being very tolerant of her.

But as Sonia went on in French, she made a mistake, and the
Frenchman corrected her; she went on in English.

Her English was louder than her French. To one person or
another she'd say, "How ridiculous! It's not like that at all! How
utterly ridiculous!" No one objected to this; it was as though she
were an overactive, perhaps frenzied relative at a big family
luncheon; everyone was used to her, and tolerant. I imagined at

times that she was saying about the luncheon itself, "How ridiculous," and no one said it wasn't, because perhaps it was.

Back in London, Sonia rang me to invite me to dinner.

I was early, and, alone in her drawing room, studied the furniture, the pictures, the books, the vase of chrysanthemums on a small, round, highly polished table which reflected the flowers. The room was bright and orderly. She came in, looking bright and orderly herself, and she moved about at quick, sharp angles as she talked.

When others arrived, she asked if I would prepare the drinks they asked for.

She introduced me as a young writer; I was twenty-five, and had published nothing. She introduced me to people whom I had known only as names, and who, I'd imagined, only existed in their names; suddenly, they had bodies—some had very large and some very small bodies—and I was drinking with them, then sitting about a round dining-room table with them. I walked home, through the clear early fall night, drunk, and imagining that the houses were books, and Sonia was opening the doors of the houses like book covers, introducing me into literary London.

At a luncheon to which I was asked by three of her old friends, they discussed happy and unhappy people; unable to say who was a really happy person, they all agreed that Sonia Orwell was the unhappiest.

A glass of wine in my hand, as I wandered about a big reception given at the Institute of Contemporary Arts, Sonia grabbed my sleeve and pulled me towards her. She said, "You must help me." Holding my sleeve, she pulled me through the crowd, in which everyone had a glass of red or white wine, to a narrow partition. She said, nodding, "There, on that side, is So-and-so with his girl friend, and there, on that side," and she nodded towards the other side, "is his wife. Now, we must talk to the wife and keep her distracted." We went. To distract the wife, I didn't have to do much; Sonia did it all.

Sonia, I thought, knew what everyone was up to.

She invited me again to her house for dinner. I arrived, just on time, with a bouquet of flowers. I kissed her and she thanked me, but when she stepped back I saw that hard look in her eyes.

Jokingly, I asked her about So-and-so and his girl friend and wife.

She said, the hardness now in her voice, "That's nothing to joke about. It's a very sad affair, a very very sad affair, and not to be treated frivolously."

"I'm sorry," I said.

My flowers in her hand, she said, "No one seems to understand what happens in human relationships, and the sadness of it all. It isn't anything to joke about. It really isn't."

I began to sweat.

The bell rang, and she answered. While she went out with the flowers, I, sweating, tried to talk, in the drawing room, with the second guest. The last time I had been here, I had been made to feel at home; now I felt constrained, and, looking at the bottles and glasses and ice cube bucket and slices of lemon, thought I mustn't presume to make myself a drink, as I didn't presume to answer when the doorbell rang again. I saw Sonia go to answer.

I wondered what had happened to my flowers.

She introduced me to the first few guests, but, as the room filled with eight or ten of us, not to others. Sometimes I stood to the side and looked into the room; sometimes I turned away to look at the pictures.

I thought: What am I doing here?

At table, I tried to take my place in the talk, but most of it—as I discovered often happened in London—had to do with people I didn't know. Whenever I did speak up, Sonia glared at me and said, "That's silly." I kept sweating. The small downstairs dining room was hot, and filled with cigarette smoke. Sonia smoked between courses. The conversation turned to a writer whose work I didn't like, and I said something about it, and Sonia said to me harshly, almost shouting, "What do you know about writing?"

With a kind of amazement, I felt myself rise up from myself and stare down at myself at the table, and that disembodied self said, coldly, "You fool."

Because I thought I must, I made efforts to be attentive and to talk, but the part of me above me stared down no matter how much I drank, and even as I walked home it said to me from above, "You stupid fool, what makes you think you have any right in that world?"

I made myself write Sonia a thank-you note.

I didn't see her for some months. As I was entering a house in Hampstead for New Year's Eve, I saw Sonia rush out from a side room to me, as though she had been waiting for me; she put out her cheeks, turning her face away, for me to kiss her, then stepped back, and spoke to me in very rapid French. For a moment, I wondered if she had mistaken me for someone else. She took me by the sleeve and pulled me into the side room, saying, all in French, that I must help her, that I would understand: at the party was a young woman who had been married to and divorced from a queer, and Sonia noticed that at the party the young woman had been talking for a long time to a nice, very straight man who showed signs of interest in her, but hadn't gone so far as to ask her for a date; I was to flirt with the young woman so the nice, very straight man would become jealous and immediately ask her for a date. "You may be American," Sonia said, "but you're French by blood, and you understand these things." I didn't want to say: Hardly. Sonia introduced me and we all sat together, Sonia and the man in armchairs, the young woman and I on a sofa. Sonia spoke without stopping. She said, "They took away the drinking laws, everyone became an alcoholic; they took away the gambling laws, and everyone became a gambler; now they're taking away the laws against homosexuals, and everyone is becoming queer." Then she jumped up, grabbed me by the hand, and pulled me out of the room, saying, "Did you hear? Did you hear? He made a date with her." I hadn't heard. Sonia took me around the rest of the party.

We saw one another often. I went to her house for luncheon, tea, drinks, dinner. I continued to meet people, some of whom became friends. Sonia came to my small flat in Battersea for dinner.

Whenever I went to Sonia's house I was apprehensive. Often, Sonia chose what I could only think of as a victim, usually a male; to whatever this guest said, Sonia responded, in French or English, "How ridiculous!" Sometimes I was the victim.

I would get home from an evening of being victimized, angry and depressed, and swear I'd never see Sonia again. The next morning, however, I'd ring her to say what a lovely dinner party she'd given, and how I longed to see her again soon.

She was able to produce in her parties an intimate sense of family reunion, as if everyone there was related and could join in the talk about those relatives who were absent. When did anyone last see So-and-so? At her house, Sonia could make one feel one had been taken into a large, peculiar family. On these evenings I would leave imagining I was a promising nephew in her large family.

We had luncheon, for the first time just the two of us together, in a small restaurant. She was talking, on and on, about a shelf in her bathroom which was on the point of collapsing. I had imagined that when I was alone with her our conversation would be intimate: we would talk about what we couldn't talk about when we were with others. Perhaps I had wanted to talk to her about what I considered most relevant to a relationship: feelings and thoughts.

I said, "I wonder if I feel more isolated here in Europe than in America."

She said, "You might as well ask if you'd feel isolated on Mars. The question doesn't have much consequence. No, no. Don't think about it." She drew in on her cigarette. "Now, I've got to get that shelf put up properly, as I have some French house guests coming."

I thought: All right, we'll talk about the shelf.

"It probably needs rawl plugs to hold it up," I said.

"Rawl plugs? What are they?"

I explained.

"How clever of you," she said. "I didn't think you were so clever. I thought there might be a reason for my liking you. And are rawl plugs difficult to put in?"

"I'd be pleased to put them in for you."

"That really is too kind. Really, really. I'd give you lunch."

We made a date for me to come to fix the falling shelf to the bathroom wall, and then I thought we'd get down to talking about what, to me, would give the luncheon its importance: I would tell Sonia a little about my inner world, and she would tell me a little about hers. But she went on talking about what else was needed for the shelf, and when we parted she said, "That was lovely," and I wondered why she thought it lovely when nothing we'd talked about, it seemed to me, had been what I considered important.

After a large lunch in her kitchen, she showed me up to the bathroom with the collapsing shelf. She had bought a box of rawl plugs, and she had as well a hand drill, a masonry bit, a hammer, a screwdriver, as I'd asked, some brand new. I thought she would leave me, but she remained in the bathroom, talking as she watched me work. When I removed the shelf, plaster dust fell from the screw holes, which were too big for the rawl plugs, but I felt I couldn't explain that, that that would have been too complicated, and, while Sonia talked, I went on working. I sweated. The shelf, when I got it up, wobbled.

Sonia said, "You are clever. Thank you so very very much."

It was as if I had done her a great service for which she would never be able to repay me.

The rawl plugs became a term of our friendship.

Sometimes I was invited to parties by people she had introduced me to, and often I would find her at the party. Once, as I entered a room, I saw Sonia standing in front of the fireplace with the painter friend at whose show I had first met her in Paris. I went to them, but Sonia, her face drawn as with the fatigue of her seriousness, was too occupied with the painter to take me in, and she turned her back a little to me. I spoke to others. When the painter left, early, I saw that Sonia was standing alone, and I went to her again. She asked me to get her another glass of wine.

I was with her the whole evening, as I felt if I left her no one else would speak to her; and, also, she spoke about the painter so obsessively there was no way to break in upon her. The painter's friend had died, perhaps killed himself, and Sonia talked about that. I kept fetching her glasses of wine, and she became very drunk. By nine-thirty, before the food was brought out, she was too drunk to stay. She was talking so quickly I imagined her talk would break through the human limits of talk and become something else. She lurched when she moved. I said I was going home, and could I give her a lift in a taxi? She followed me out. In the taxi, she went on talking, in a higher and higher pitched, accusing voice, about how unhappy the painter was.

"You don't understand," she said. "None of you understands what desperation is. You won't help. I could kill, kill, kill, kill, kill, kill you all for your lack of sensitivity. He is suffering. Does any one of you care? Do you ring him up? Fuck all if you do."

I had to contain my anger, and, getting out of the taxi, showed her to her door to make sure she got in. It was about ten o'clock, and instead of returning to the party I went home, feeling that, as I did not understand real desperation, I understood nothing. Sonia did understand.

I asked her to a dinner party to which I'd asked people I hadn't met through her, people she didn't know, or hardly knew. She arrived early; she'd been to a drinks party and was drunk. I gave her more to drink, and she, laughing in a hard, dry way, her head thrown back, told me she hadn't wanted to come to a dinner party, had wanted to go home and to bed. As she laughed, I laughed, my laughter as hard and dry as hers. She said, "I hate dinner parties," and laughed. I laughed.

I drank a lot.

A woman novelist came. Sonia was very attentive to her, and the moment the novelist put a cigarette between her lips, Sonia jumped across the room with a lit cigarette lighter for her.

They talked, as if alone, about queers.

The novelist said, "I don't trust them."

"I know exactly what you mean," Sonia said. "Let me tell you about queers." She laughed.

I laughed. I said, "Stop it."

Sonia said to me, "You listen to us. There are a few things you should know."

I said, "Why don't we talk about Jews?"

The other guests came: a male novelist, his lady friend, a television producer, an Irish tenor.

I said, "Thank God you've come."

"Why?" the male novelist asked.

"They were ganging up to talk about nothing but queers."

We all laughed, hard, dry laughter.

I gave everyone drinks.

To get off the subject of queers, I congratulated the male writer on a book he had recently published.

Sonia said, "I won't read it. I'm sure it's awful."

We all laughed.

More hysterical than anyone, I was incoherent, kept knocking over glasses, and tripping as I served food. In my small room, we were crowded together about the gas fire, on chairs and my bed, eating from our laps.

And all the while Sonia talked, talked more rapidly than I have heard anyone else talk, ever. The others were silent.

Sonia stopped for a moment, there was a pause, and I thought: I'll just go and leave them all here to fate as there's nothing I can do.

She said to the tenor, "Will you sing some Irish songs with something about liberty in them?"

I thought: I must go. If they don't all go now, I must.

The tenor sang, his face raised and his eyes closed, medieval Irish songs, and after he finished the silence was terrible.

In a burst, Sonia gave a history of Ireland from 1169 or some such early date, which went on and on, all jumbled. She involved Israel in Irish history, and her pro-Irish sentiments gave way to pro-Israeli sentiments. She had flipped her lid. Nothing, I thought, could put it back on.

The only person she looked at, intently, was the woman novelist. Sonia kept jumping up to light her cigarettes.

When Sonia paused, I asked the male novelist if he would sing. He did. He sang "Jerusalem".

I asked others to sing. The television producer did.

I sang "The Battle Hymn of the Republic".

Sonia refused to sing, as did the other women.

All the guests left at exactly ten o'clock.

While I cleared up the plates, glasses, overfilled ashtrays, I felt sick. I went to bed.

Two days later, I went to Sonia's for dinner. I was worried that the evening she had spent with me would in ways I couldn't imagine be continued. The female novelist was there.

Sonia put me on her right. She spoke calmly. That there was no hysteria about her almost disappointed me. Everyone else was calm too.

Over dessert, Sonia said to me, "I feel I was too rowdy at your flat the other evening. I'm very sorry about it. I was drunk."

I said, "I thought you were spirited."

"I was nervous," she said. "I always lose control when I'm with people I don't know."

The evening was a bright family evening, and, again, I felt that Sonia gave me a place in that family; she made me feel that I belonged in London. For her, as for me, any family in London was a made-up family; she was entirely devoted to it.

I had a vision of Sonia giving or going out to, every day, luncheons, teas, drinks, dinners. But I saw that these required as great an effort when she went out to them as when she received; I think she often hated them.

I felt this: that what she really wanted was to lie on her bed in a darkened room.

More and more, she said, "Ridiculous! Ridiculous!"

That *ridiculous* became a state of the world. I could not imagine that there was some particular trouble in Sonia's life which gave rise to such a general condemnation because Sonia would not allow me to imagine it. Whatever it might have been she kept it to herself, but there were outward signs of something kept in. She seemed to become physically uncoordinated, and sometimes, going into or out of a restaurant, tripped. Once, she fell in her house and hurt her jaw and lower lip so she had to have stitches. A tiny vein, like a fine, bright red worm, appeared just inside a nostril. She became prone to infections: a toe, a tooth. If I asked her how she was, she laughed and said, "Awful," but that was all about herself. She'd quickly start talking about something else.

I realized that Sonia made me aware that everything I said and did, my very tone of voice and gestures, was vain. When I was with her her effect was to make me see my life as meaningless, as I knew she saw her own life. She did not impose this on me; it happened by my being in her presence. I could have decided not to be a friend of hers, but I was, I think, a close friend (she introduced me to others as a close friend); I wanted to be a close friend perhaps because I felt she saw the truth, and I respected her for seeing it. I would think: She's right, everything is ridiculous.

Then she'd say to me, "Life being life, which is awful, of course we've got to be friends and help one another. *Of course.*"

She helped her friends in need as if she, herself, had no need of help.

When a friend died, she seemed not to grieve. I think she grieved privately, and the only evidence I had of that was when she stated in a direct way that she had been weeping all the night before. Her eyes looked swollen. But other than her stating this there was no way I could get her to talk about what she had wept for. I knew that if I did try to talk to her about her grief, she would, harshly, tell me I didn't understand.

There were weeks when I didn't see her; I had become used to seeing her weekly. If I rang her in the late morning, her voice sounded as if I'd just woken her. If I rang her in the late afternoon, she sounded as if she were about to go to bed.

When we did meet, she'd say, "I haven't seen anyone in a long time. I couldn't. I simply couldn't."

I wanted to help her, as she would have helped me; but when I said, "Please let me know if I can do anything," she smiled, then frowned.

A friend did go to stay with Sonia to care for her. In the late morning, she'd bring a tray up to her, and would either find Sonia in a darkened room, her head lifted a little from the pillow, saying angrily, "You fucking well woke me just when I'd fallen asleep," or, in a bright room, sitting up in bed, saying, as she stubbed out her cigarette in an ashtray, "*Enfin*. I thought breakfast would never come."

We wondered what was wrong with Sonia.

Then, unexpectedly, she sold her house, and a short time after she moved to Paris. There was something manic in the move, as if Paris were a solution to a problem which had no other solution. She told the newspapers that she was going to get a job reading and translating for a French publisher.

In Paris, she remained in close touch with her friends in London. We discussed her when we met. No one understood quite why she was living in Paris in what appeared to be self-imposed exile: she did not seem to have a job with a publisher; she did not seem to be seeing her French friends; she was in Paris for no apparent reason.

2

SHE AND I corresponded. Her letters were affectionate, and as if filled with small fresh bunches of flowers.

But I was worried about Sonia, and, in a letter, asked her if she'd like to join me the coming summer in Italy, where I was part-owner of a stone house in the mountains. I'm not sure I expected her to take me up. She did, and I wondered if I'd made a mistake.

There were lots of letters and telephone conversations between us about Italy.

She was to drive down from Paris and meet me in the South of France, where I had gone to stay with members of her London 'family'.

My host said to me, "Poor thing, going to Italy with Sonia."

"She seemed lonely in Paris," I answered. "I thought I'd try to help her. But I'm worried that everything will go wrong in Italy."

"Well," he said, "if she doesn't like it she can leave quickly enough. She'll say, '*Zut alors*,' and she'll be off."

His wife said, "The boss will be tough, but, you'll see, you can count on her being helpful."

One afternoon before Sonia arrived an American writer came to tea, which we had under the mulberry tree. When I said I was going to Italy with Sonia Orwell, she said, "You're out of your fucking mind."

Sonia arrived from Paris in great heat, sweating. Instead of sitting in the shade and having cold white wine, however, she picked up the hostess's secateurs and went into the garden. After a while, the hostess and I went to look for her and found her cutting away at a rose plant, flinging the cuttings out on to the gravel. We stopped at a distance and simply watched her. Quietly, I said, "In Italy, I think I'll let her do exactly what she wants."

Whenever Sonia and I met one another, outside or inside the house, she'd say, "We must talk about our trip," then walk away as though she didn't want to talk about it. She always carried her handbag. I'd say, meeting her, "We should at least study maps," and she'd throw her head back and say, "Oh, maps!" and walk away, her bag held by its strap, as if she were on her way, in a hurry, to a specific place where she had to do something much more important than discuss maps with me; then she'd stop ten feet away, suddenly uncertain where she was going, turn and say, "No, maps are essential, we must have maps." She'd then go off in another direction with her bag, stop, not sure where she should go, and go off in still another direction.

In the afternoon, we settled with tea and maps, and Sonia asked me if I would ring a garage in Rapallo—the point on our route at which, she calculated, she would have driven her new car 3,000 miles, so would have to have it serviced. She could not speak Italian. I rang the French operator in Marseilles to place the call. The connection was bad. The operator said, "I can't hear you. You've got to speak louder." I shouted. She said, "Speak louder. Where are you?" I shouted more, "But I'm shouting! Bouches du Rhône!" She said, "Well, I don't understand. It's obvious you don't speak French." A fury passed through me. I shouted, "*I* speak French! *You* don't understand French!" She said, in that matter-of-fact way, "If you don't speak French—" I slammed the receiver down. I was trembling, angry not only with the telephonist, with all of France, but angry that Sonia should have heard me.

She said, "I'm glad I overheard that. I didn't know you were capable of getting angry in that way. It's a revelation and, in a strange way, it'll make travelling with you easier."

I wondered, then, if she was worried about travelling with me.

I said, "I'll try ringing again in an hour."

We went back to our tea and the maps which Sonia continued to study closely.

With a pencil on the edge of the map she made a calculation.

"Wait," she said, "wait. I've got a nought too many. The car doesn't have to be serviced."

I learned that Sonia was very bad at calculations.

Exhausted, Sonia nevertheless helped to prepare dinner.

The next day, she, our host and I went to see the Roman ruins at Glanum. It began to rain, and we stood under a tin roof which protected a mosaic. The ruins—great stone slabs, blocks, columns, carved pediments on the ground—went black in the wet.

Sonia was silent when we got back and sat in the living room drinking tea. Our friends played Scrabble. Sonia's silence frightened me a little, and I tried to get her to talk by asking her questions about Paris; but, as I couldn't presume to ask her specific questions about her life the questions were general, and she answered them in brief though absolute comments about Parisians, whom she believed to be the most civilized people in the world. I knew I was straining my attention towards her; I couldn't bear her silence, and I felt it was my responsibility to bring her out of it. But I knew, too, that she would resent my imagining I had that responsibility. I saw Sonia as an unspeakably unhappy woman. I was in love with the unhappiness in her, and yet reassured that, no matter what I did, what I felt it my duty to do, to lessen that unhappiness, I couldn't: Sonia wouldn't allow me to. Sonia reassured me in her frightening unhappiness. It was her secret.

After a silence, she asked me how many bedrooms there were in the house in Italy. I said three. "Then we can ask others if they'd like to join us," she said, her voice all at once spirited. "Of course," I said, and thought: She wants others to join us, she doesn't want to be alone there with me. "Ask anyone you'd like," I said. I, too, was suddenly spirited. Perhaps I didn't want to be alone with Sonia; and yet I was dispirited at the same time, as though she had found me in some way inadequate, immature. She asked our hostess if she might use the telephone, and rang three friends in London, proposing to each in turn that he should come to Italy; each friend said it wasn't possible. The friends were members of her London family, without whom I imagined Sonia felt completely alone. I was not enough of that family to make her feel contained by it. With me she seemed to feel exposed to a world she was uncertain of entering, and I had the momentary impression, when she came back from the telephone to sit at the other end of the sofa from me, that she resented my making her do what threatened her; but it was too late to draw back.

The night before we left for Italy, she took a sleeping pill. Her room was next to mine, and I heard her turning listlessly in bed, getting up often to open or shut her window.

We left early Sunday morning before our friends woke.

It was hot, and the empty Provençal roads glared.

There was no traffic until we were diverted from the *autoroute* and had to go over the Grande Corniche, where the cars were jammed up against one another. Sonia became ill-tempered. She said, "This is just what I didn't want to happen, but, of course, it would." It occurred to me that Sonia's most constant temper was ill temper. What I had to hope for was that, after this, everything would be all right so she wouldn't have any reason to be ill-tempered, but I knew that, of course, nothing would be right. Sonia was naturally ill-tempered, as if just having to live, day after day, were reason enough.

I thought ahead to the house, which was very simple, as I had told her. It had doors and windows, electricity and water, and beds. She said it sounded as though it had everything one needed. I told her that the summer before I'd arranged with a local contractor to whitewash the inside walls, but I was sure that hadn't been done; no work was done, ever, when I wasn't there. She said that didn't matter. I didn't tell her that I imagined the house, closed up all winter, would have broken windowpanes, cobwebs, dirt, and the bodies of dead birds and little animals all over the floors.

Once we crossed the border into Italy, I felt that I was responsible to Sonia for the entire country, but I would not be able to do anything to make the country pleasant.

There was with Sonia the sense that she knew beforehand everything that was going to happen, and there would be no great surprises; everything would be awful.

At lunchtime we turned off the *autostrada* into an ugly modern seaside town. I asked a man selling water-melons by the side of the road where we could eat well, and he pointed across a flat, bare area strewn with old bags of hardened cement and automobile tires to a group of stern cement apartment buildings.

Sonia parked the car with difficulty (as it was a new car she was very careful with it), and for a moment was irritated and frowned deeply; but as we walked over the field to the restaurant, in the bottom of one of the apartment blocks, I saw she became a little, a very little, excited. Part of her excitement, I was sure, was that the restaurant was working class. It was crowded, but a large, dark, blunt-looking man invited us to join him at his table, where he was alone. He offered us some of his wine.

Studying Sonia, he said, "You were born in August."

"Yes," she said, smiling at him.

"You're a Virgo."

She smiled more, with that smile which suddenly, unexpectedly, parted her lips and teeth, drew back her cheeks, and opened her eyes wide.

She said to me, "Ask him what sign he is."

"Scorpio," he said.

"I wouldn't have known," Sonia said.

(I was reminded that Sonia was very good at reading palms.)

The Italian said, "My two interests are astrology and driving fast around curves. I drive around curves with passion."

They talked about astrology and driving.

Big, dark, blunt-featured as he was, he was gentle, even delicate in his words and manners towards Sonia, who, herself, became gentle and delicate. She laughed lightly.

As we walked back to the car across the field, I noted that Sonia's face retained an openness, as from the pleasure of meeting what she called a really European and civilized working-class man.

I knew that she would, from the encounter, imagine she had an insight into the working class in Italy.

I thought: Italy interests her.

We stopped for petrol, and, waiting, watched a man pay out a stack of thousand-lire notes, one at a time, to the garage man; the stack was about six inches thick, and the man counted them out slowly.

Sonia's narrowed eyes expressed a barely suppressed impatience; her whole face narrowed.

I thought: Italy bores her.

She found it exhausting to drive in and out of the tunnels through the mountains along the Ligurian coast.

She became exhausted quickly.

In Lucca, where we decided to stop for the night, there was

only a double room in the main hotel. When I told Sonia this I wondered, for a moment, if she might say we could share the room. I thought to myself: I wouldn't mind. She said nothing. I quickly rang friends who lived in the hills outside Lucca to ask them to recommend another hotel, and they said, "Come here, you'll cheer us up." I was worried, as we drove off to find the villa, that Sonia, there, would get drunk. I lost the way, and Sonia said, "Now I can't try every fucking road in Italy." I said, "Turn left." It was the right turn.

As we were driving off in the morning she said, "I was so frightened on my way there. Was I all right? I always think that, especially with people I don't know, I'm going to say or do something awful." I said, "You were marvellous. I know they liked you very much." Sonia said, "I'm like that woman in a short story by Chekhov who knows she is about to say something awful, and tries to stop herself, but can't. You're quite sure I wasn't awful?" "I promise you," I said. She frowned deeply.

Driving up the mountain into the walled town of Cortona, I said, "I love this place."

Sonia herself hardly expressed in person the warm emotions she expressed in letters, but she liked people with her to express emotions—of course, towards other people, places, things, and never towards herself. Feelings expressed to her for her made her angry.

I wanted her to like Cortona. As we walked down the narrow medieval main street in the high bright coolness after the flat heat of the plain, she said nothing. I did not know if she was impressed by the town or not.

(Later, she told me she hated it.)

In a restaurant, we had a lunch of roast pigeons, then we started on the drive into the mountains to the house. I thought: Oh God, the road's so long, so winding, and what state will the house be in? I saw her face become more and more set, her eyes more and more narrow the more curves we took. Once she said, "I think I took that curve with passion." I wondered then if she were in fact having a good time and joking, or if she were angry.

We got out of the car by the river, crossed the rickety bridge, went up the path. The house was half hidden by weeds; a part of the roof of the pergola had fallen. I looked at Sonia, who, I imagined, winced.

The first comment Sonia made was, inside the house, "It's filthy dirty, and I can't live in filth."

I didn't think it was filthy.

She immediately got out a bucket from beneath the kitchen sink and filled it with water, then took up a broom and a thick, rough floor rag. The sleeves of her pink smock rolled up and wet, she shoved the rag about the tile floors with the broom.

"What a holiday," she said.

I thought she would become more angry if I apologized.

We had a silent supper and went to bed early. She got up early, and I heard her in the kitchen. I lay in bed wondering if she'd be in a bad temper. I got up and found her preparing coffee. In a slightly hoarse voice she said, "You know, I woke this morning at dawn and looked out of the window of my bedroom, and I thought, This is one of the most beautiful places in the world. Then I looked around the house and I thought, This *could* be a very pretty house."

She found herself in a situation that was unpleasant to her, I thought, if not unbearable, and her only way of making it, not pleasant, but bearable, was to help make the house pretty.

I followed behind her writing out a list as she went through the rooms showing me what had to be done: curtains here, cushions there, a table here, walls whitewashed.

The contractor came with a huge demijohn of wine on the back of a tractor. I embraced him. Sonia said, "Is this the man responsible for redoing the house?" "Yes," I said. She lit a cigarette, put one foot forward, and frowned at him. Sonia said, "Then tell him—" and she made me repeat, in Italian, everything she found wrong: cracks in the plaster, a windowpane broken, electric outlets in the wrong places, on and on. He was stunned. He left quickly, and didn't come back all the while Sonia was there.

I decanted the wine into large two-litre bottles, and Sonia and I began to drink.

She said, "Well, the wine is lovely. It's light, and one can drink and drink it without any worry."

We drank bottle after bottle of it as we discussed what had to be done to the house; she repeated her list obsessively, and I agreed.

Then we went out, the next few days, to buy furniture. I had some money. We bought a dining-room table, a *madia*, and we drove off to the Zona Industriale because someone had said there one could find good cheap chairs, but Sonia thought they were too expensive, and, after days of looking, she finally allowed me to buy six chairs from a wholesale dealer. She made me buy material for cushions, kapok, a big cooking pot, a salad basket. She had me make, each morning, a list: lining paper for drawers, drawing pins, towel rails, a new broom. Often, I thought the items weren't necessary, but I put them on the list. She insisted I go and ask the widow in the next farm if she'd help clean the house, which she would, and if her son Candido would sickle away the weeds and restore the pergola and do some whitewashing of walls. At lunch and supper, always with big bottles of wine, we talked of nothing but the house. I sometimes found her replacing dim bulbs with brighter ones, polishing a table top. She was always active for the house; when, seldom, we sat out in deck chairs under the pergola in the evening and continued to drink wine, she talked about the house, as if, even in her talk, she were obsessively active.

She was of course always exhausted.

There were times, looking at the house through Sonia's eyes, when I hated it.

One Saturday afternoon, while I was whitewashing the up-stairs sitting room with Candido, an American friend who lived up the valley came in. Candido was on top of a ladder which was on a table, and the American just under him. The ladder slipped, Candido fell into the American's arms, and the bucket of whitewash on top of both of them. Sonia ran upstairs to see what had happened. Downstairs in the kitchen, she filled a tub of water and told the American and Candido to take off their clothes so she could wash them. While the American and Candido were in their underpants, Sonia washing their shirts and trousers in the tub, I pouring out wine, an aged Italian neighbour arrived, mopping his neck and face with a white towel, and carrying, in a knotted bandana, a bottle of wine, a loaf of bread, and about two kilos of sausages. He had come to welcome us to Italy.

I introduced Sonia to him as *la zia*, which she liked. She kept calling herself *la zia*.

The old man's politeness impressed her. She liked politeness.

When, in the freshly whitewashed sitting room, I began to put out a kelim and pillows, Sonia rushed in. She said, "I knew it. I knew you were doing the fun part without me." She told me which way to lay out the kelim, where to place the pillows.

There were, I thought, spirited moments.

We went off to Città di Castello for the morning market. She said to me, "You don't know me in the market." It sounded like a threat. I had to run after her as she went from stall to stall, still buying for the house. Her way of getting the price down was to pick up something—a ladle—look at it, frown deeply, put it down, and half turn away. The man in the stall would lower the price, and Sonia would say to me, quickly, "Buy it." We had a long lunch, and ate dishes we had never had before, and we drank a lot of the light local wine she liked so much. Outside the restaurant, I turned in one direction, Sonia in another. I said, "This is the way." "No," she said, "this is." I insisted, she insisted. "All right," she said, "you go your way, I'll go mine, and we'll see who gets to the car first." I was determined to get there first, and raced through the empty, sun-filled streets; when I turned a corner, I saw Sonia leaning back, one hand on the car, one on her hip, and as I went to her she tossed back her head and smiled at me.

But even the small spirited moments seemed to me to rise out of and bring Sonia back to a sense of something vast and unspirited which had to be endured.

When she wasn't working on or for the house, she read, in the hammock strung up under the pergola, a book by an American woman who lived near by. On our way to have lunch with this woman in a restaurant in Cortona, I saw that Sonia was worried as usual about meeting someone she didn't know. We arrived first, and I ordered wine before anything else; I knew with the wine and her cigarettes Sonia would feel a little secure. She was drunk when the writer came in. I introduced them, then sat tensely, listening. The writer mentioned friends of hers whom she assumed to be friends of Sonia's. Sonia said, "They're swine." "Oh, come now," the writer said. I tensed more, and thought: Well, you can always write about this later. But I saw that the writer's authoritative "Oh, come now" made Sonia sit back; it was as if she had recognized, in a moment, the strength of the other woman, and was, in that moment, reassured by it. Sonia, I realized, deferred to women stronger than she. I saw in her face that she liked the American woman suddenly, and that the luncheon was going to be a success. I relaxed and listened to them talk on and on. Sonia nervously drank a great deal, and smoked cigarettes one after the other, but she didn't, as she would have if her nervousness had gone out of her control, talk without stop. The two women embraced before Sonia and I went off, back into the mountains.

She was very drunk, but she insisted on driving the tight curves. Her concentration, it seemed to me, centred more and more, not on the curves, but something that made her increasingly angry.

Back at the house, she continued to drink. She insisted on helping with supper, a chicken casserole. She drank as she helped. She drank through the meal.

All the while her anger, I felt, was growing.

After supper she went up to her room to put on her nightgown and housecoat and slippers, and pull her hair to the top of her head with an elastic band, and came downstairs again. As I sat at the cleared table, she, drinking out of a greasy glass, walked up and down the room, sometimes pulling at her hair.

She said, "You've been wanting this conversation. I haven't. But as you want it, I'll tell you what I think about you. I'm not interested in getting to know you any better than I do now, though I suspect you want to get to know me better. Well, I'll tell you one thing about myself: I'm not as frivolous as you think I am. You think I'm frivolous. I'm not. And I'll tell you this about yourself, though you may not want to hear it: you are. And I'll tell you the difference. I think. What you don't do is think. I do *think*. You don't think. I like being among the French because they *think*. Why don't you *think*!"

I thought: Well, it's true, I can't think. But I tried to tell her that I didn't trust thinking, that writing, I believed, didn't come from drawing conclusions.

She shouted, "Conclusions! There *are* no conclusions! You

don't understand. You'll never understand. I'm talking about good hard thinking, about thinking things through, about seeing something in every possible way. You won't be a good writer until you can think things through."

I said, "If thinking is seeing a person in order to block off every part of him and name it, I'm against thinking, because I have to believe there are parts of a person which can't be blocked off and named—"

She exploded. "Against thinking! How can you say that? What do you think thinking is? Naming? Do you think it's what Freddy Ayer thinks? My God, my God. *Freddy Ayer. He doesn't think*. You don't understand about thinking. You *are* frivolous. Your writing is frivolous. It isn't thought through. I do think. I do think things through. I'm not frivolous. You were a Catholic. You studied syllogisms. You know about the displaced middle. So was I a Catholic. I learned what good hard thinking is. Why are you frivolous, and I'm not? Is it because you're American? You Americans. You Americans. We Europeans know how to think. When you told me the other day that you wanted to write a beautiful book, I thought, No real writer would say that, because that's a frivolous reason for writing a book. How *could* you have said that? Freddy Ayer. *Freddy Ayer*. My God. I know Freddy Ayer. I know he doesn't think. How can you imagine that thinking is what Freddy Ayer thinks? How *could* you say you want to write a beautiful book and consider yourself a serious writer? I find it hard to believe you are a serious writer. And I'll tell you there are a number of people who think the same. Jean Rhys tells me you're a writer. I have to believe her. But a lot of others tell me you're not. They, like me, know that you lack thinking. My God, my God. Freddy Ayer."

I was angry, and I sat, silent, thinking: What am I doing here listening to this obsessed woman?

"And another thing I've got to tell you," she shouted. "You're frivolous because you're worldly. Yes, you must be a part of the world if you're going to write about it, but you're too much a part of it, too much taken in by it. You lead a very chic life. The people you invite to your house are very worldly people. You'd be surprised that in Paris I have very very ordinary friends. You imagine I see only grand friends. It's not true. I'm not so worldly.

I see perfectly ordinary people in Paris and we think things through in our talk. No, you're too worldly. All you talk about is Germaine Greer."

My anger began to give way to depression.

She went on. "I didn't want to tell you these things, but you wanted me to. You'll ruin yourself by being worldly."

"Yes," I said dully.

Her obsession lasted till four o'clock in the morning. I simply said, from time to time, "Yes," and became, with each yes, more depressed. I imagined us as from a great distance, in a dimly lit stone house in a dark valley.

"You don't know about life and death," she said; "you don't, you haven't thought your way through living and dying, and the awfulness of both."

In bed, I lay thinking: Why do I imagine Sonia is a close friend? Though I might have tried to think it through, whatever made her a friend, and a close friend, would have to have been, literally, unthinkable.

The next day we were both very quiet. The woman writer came over in the late afternoon to ask us if we would like to join her for dinner. Sonia said she couldn't, she was too exhausted. I thought for a moment I might go, but I said I'd stay. After the writer left, I lit the fire in the *scaldabagno* so Sonia could have her bath. We were quiet again.

With our first glasses of wine, I said to Sonia, "I have an idea. Let's make a little excursion for a few days to the hill towns."

Her narrowed eyes opened, and the small wrinkles of her face were pulled back as her face, too, appeared to open. She smiled. "What a good idea," she said.

My idea was to get her away from the house.

We set off over the Umbrian mountains towards Urbino. She was concentrating tensely on the roads. I, too, was tense with concentration, and, even when I passed her a cigarette and her lighter, stared with Sonia at the road which sometimes doubled back on itself, at steeper and steeper angles.

In Urbino, I found a good, clean hotel, and I saw on Sonia's face, as she entered the bright marble-floored foyer, a look of relief.

In the Ducal Palace, which she said she thought the most beautiful building in the world, I imagined her looking at the spaces, those clean, bright spaces, as with longing. In room after room, we were silent; she kept walking away from me to a window, a far doorway, her back turned to me. I let her go on ahead, and followed at a distance.

In the evening, we sat out in the café in the main square. We didn't talk for long, still periods.

When, about nine o'clock, she said she was tired and rose to go to the hotel, she leaned towards me and said, "Don't pick anyone up." She wasn't joking. I said, "Do you think I would?" "Thanks for that," she said, and left.

I remained in the café in the piazza. The air was warm and smelled of the perspiration of the people crowded about me at other tables. I felt very much alone, and I wondered why, if I felt so alone with Sonia, I wanted to be with her. Why was I drawn to a woman—and, when I considered it, to women—who made me feel so isolated, and made me question myself body and soul? Of course I was drawn to her for her literary world, in which I'd wanted a place. Here, however, we were both outside that world. I was drawn to her, more, for what I imagined to be her reason for having to have a world of friends about her to whom she could devote herself: for that deep darkness in her which she seemed to accept as a fact nothing could be done about, and which made her turn away from herself and it to her friends. Sonia made me aware that I, as she, was entirely isolated; in her case, she denied the importance—the selfish, or, she might have said, the self-indulgent importance—of such isolation, but I was nevertheless attracted to that isolation more than to her deliberate, disinterested devotion to friends.

I realized my whole attitude towards Sonia had been sentimental and selfish: I had been drawn to her darkness because she, who commanded a place in the world, was justified in her darkness, and justified mine. I had perhaps even imagined that, alone with her in Italy, I would try to get her, in some subtle way, to commiserate with me for my isolating darkness, though I could not imagine Sonia taking me in her arms. This, of course, was ridiculous; all those dark, isolating feelings had to be kept inside, because there was nothing that could be done about them;

they had to be kept secret. It occurred to me that, for years and years, I had assumed that the deepest feelings one could have were the darkest, and that the deepest relationship one could have with another person was in communicating those darkest feelings to him or her, to understand them and to have them understood. I had presumed the world to be, somehow, inside—a world of privileged friends who communicated to one another their inner feelings and thoughts, mostly rather sad feelings and thoughts. But the only world that mattered, I saw now, was the world outside one's thoughts and feelings, and friends communicated with one another in terms of that world—not talking to one another about feelings and thoughts, but helping one another to put their houses in order. Never would I be able to talk to Sonia about feelings and thoughts—her own even less than mine—and that, I knew, was right; Sonia was right not to talk about what didn't matter, but to do what one had to do to get on.

Perhaps, I told myself, I had learned something from her, though it would have been very difficult to articulate exactly what. As with the sense of accomplishing something for the first time, thinking out something thoroughly, I left the café and walked across the traffic-less piazza to the hotel.

Sonia was difficult, but she was difficult for a reason. She wanted, demanded so much from herself and from others, and it made her rage that she and others couldn't ever match what was done to what was aspired to. I admired her for being difficult. I could admire her like this when I wasn't with her.

In the hill towns, we stayed in clean, bright hotels. Sonia relaxed and slept well.

Back in Cortona, I rang the writer, who invited us to dinner and to spend the night with her. The two women talked animatedly while I said nothing. I left them talking and drinking and went to bed.

At my house in the morning, Sonia immediately got on her hands and knees to pull up the weeds that had grown among the paving stones under the pergola and began to talk about the outside of the house: a row of oleanders there, the lilacs cut back there—

Before going to bed, I said, "Sonia, if you'd like to get away from the house tomorrow, the Saturday market is on in Cortona."

"I'm not sure," she said.

"Only if you'd like."

In the early morning, I heard her get up. I got up.

"We'll go to the market," she said.

While Sonia wandered about the stalls in the small stone squares of the town, I did chores. In the post office I stood in a queue behind a woman I thought I recognized; I leaned forward and did recognize her, an American professor of literature who lived in England. Surprised, I asked her what she was doing in Cortona, and she, as if there were no reason at all to be surprised, said, "I'm staying at Germaine Greer's." She said that as she was buying and preparing lunch at Germaine's she thought she could ask me along. I said, "I'm with Sonia Orwell. I'll have to ask her. She may say no, she doesn't want to go to Germaine's." I went out into the market and found Sonia buying many tiny handkerchiefs from a woman standing before a big cardboard box full of them; I brought her back to the American professor, who invited Sonia, and Sonia said, "That *would* be lovely." I thought: Oh God, Sonia and Germaine, and I recalled their first brief encounter. I said to Sonia, "Only if you *want* to go." She answered, "Of course I *want* to go." I did not want to go.

I did a few more chores, then Sonia and I drove off. On the dusty white roads, I got lost. I saw her frowning. When I found my way, up a narrow rocky road, I saw her frown more. I said, "Remember, this whole escapade is not my responsibility." She said nothing. The car bounced over ruts, and she winced. I said, "We can go back. I'm very willing to go back." "No," she said, "if it doesn't get any worse." "It does get worse," I said. Sonia drove on a little further over ruts. "We'll park the car by the side of the road," she said, "and walk." "It's a long walk," I said. "We'll do it," she said.

I thought: She *wants* to see Germaine.

We walked up a steep road in white heat for about a kilometre. Sonia didn't talk. Her hair began to drip with sweat.

I repeated, "We could go back."

"We'll go on."

Through the chestnut trees, I saw the red tile roof of the house.

We approached by way of the garden of all-white flowers. Germaine, under the fig tree before the house, stood with one hand on her throat, another on her thrust-out hip. She was wearing a red dress and blue high-heeled shoes. As I went to her, she said in a loud voice, "My guests invited guests to lunch without asking me first." I didn't take in what she said, but, laughing, kissed her on both cheeks. She drew back and gave me a glinting look. She said, "My guests do what they like in my house." I took it in suddenly, and just as suddenly became angry. I thought: I'm going. But when I looked round at Sonia, sweating and leaning forward with exhaustion, I thought: I'll have to be polite. The professor came out and Germaine went in. Sonia talked with the American in a loud voice, saying, over and over, "What a beautiful place this is. And the all-white garden was obviously planted by a genius. What a spot." Germaine leaned out of a window and said to Sonia, "Would you like a glass of white wine, dear?" Sonia went into the house with the professor, and I heard the women speaking.

From another room, I heard the professor's husband trying to quieten their crying children so they would sleep.

Still depressed, I lay in the hammock and closed my eyes.

After lunch, just before Sonia and I left, Germaine took me up behind her house to, she said, show me what wild thyme looked like, as I'd said I'd never seen any. Both of us leaning over a low plant of wild thyme, she said, "I'm sorry. I don't want to have guests now." I said, "If you invite guests, you must bear them. I thought you above all would insist on that." "Why above all me?" she asked. I said, "Because I thought you knew about responsibility." She pursed her lips, lowered her eyes, put the knuckles of her index fingers to her cheeks, and pretended to cry.

Sonia was drunk. All the way down to the car she talked about what had happened. Sometimes she stumbled on the stones and ruts.

I kept thinking how she, in an instant, had taken complete control of the situation as if as a responsibility, as if she had realized she, as a duty, must save the luncheon. She had had to drink a lot to do it, and she had talked in the silences with a kind of passion to do it, but she had succeeded.

On the way to the car, she said, "It was my fault, Germaine's reaction, I know it was."

"I'm sure it wasn't."

"Yes, I'm sure it was," she said.

I said, "Oh, Sonia."

"I like Germaine," she said. "Her house revealed a lot about her I liked. It's an entirely feminine house."

"Yes."

In the car, before starting off, she said, "I want to be a good person, but I'm not."

I did not know what to say.

"Most people don't like me," she said.

From Germaine's we went, for tea, to the house of an Oxford graduate student, who had a number of other students staying with him. On the terrace, Sonia was given a chair under a big umbrella, and the students sat around her. Instead of tea, Sonia was given cold white wine. I had to go off to collect chairs which had been re-caned, and when I returned I found Sonia, with waves of an arm and backward thrusts of her head, pronouncing on various writers she knew whom the students asked her about.

"Oh, I can tell you about—"

The students stared at her with wonder.

Back in the car, she said, "I did it again. I put on my act, my widow of George Orwell act. Was I awful? I'm so drunk. Did they think I was a fool?"

I said, "They were fascinated."

She drove carefully. She insisted on preparing supper, which she did drunkenly, but carefully.

As she went upstairs to bed, she said, "I hated today, but in a way I'm glad for all of it. I hate everything, but, finally, I have to be glad for it all."

Her last day with me was bright and clear and fresh. I did not know what mood Sonia was in. She went on her own for a walk, and returned with a huge bunch of wild flowers which she arranged in a pitcher. Then she wandered off again. She seemed to wander, out of and into the house, throughout the day.

3

SONIA CAME BACK to London more and more often from Paris on what she called business trips, trips to see her lawyer about a lawsuit (or lawsuits) she would only talk about when drunk, and then so incoherently one couldn't understand except for the great importance of it (or them) to her. She said, "Once I win—and I've put everything I've got into winning—I'll kill myself." There was a sense one got from her during these business trips that she was unable to explain her legal problems because they, complex as they were, had to do with something more complex in Sonia, which she did not want to go into—which she could not go into. Her drunken attempts to describe her litigation always ended with her saying, "It's all much much more complicated than can be imagined, and much much more awful. It's desperate."

I went to Paris to visit her. She asked me, please, to come to lunch, to supper, to lunch the next day.

Nothing was going right for her.

She lived in a narrow, L-shaped room in a low building, like a cottage, at the back of an alley. There was a small kitchen and a bathroom off the kitchen where the air smelled slightly of escaping gas. She met friends in expensive restaurants, where she insisted, always, on paying the large bills.

In a dim restaurant—decorated with chamber pots on shelves—I said, "It must be wonderful living in Paris."

"You don't understand Paris," she said.

"No, I don't."

"Even I don't understand Paris. I'm a foreigner, and I realize I don't, after all, speak French very well."

"Will you stay?"

"I've got to stay."

When the waiter came to the table to ask if there was anything we wanted, she shouted at him, "*Laissez nous en paix*," and he, startled, stepped back and said, '*Tres bien*, madame." She said to me, "Why did I do that? Why? Yesterday a young woman stopped me in the street to ask me the time, and I shouted at her, 'Do you think I can give the time to everyone who stops me in the street?' Afterwards, I wondered why I'd been so rude to her. Why? Why am I so filled with anger?"

I said nothing.

She said, "I've fucked up my life. I'm angry because I've fucked up my life."

When I kissed her goodbye before getting into a taxi, I saw there were tears in her eyes.

In London, I visited her painter friend to talk about her. I felt a need to talk about Sonia with her friends. I sat with him at one end of a long room; bare bulbs hung on wires from the low ceiling. I asked him if Sonia had ever attacked him, as she attacked so many of her friends.

"No," he said, "she never has."

"Why, I wonder."

He thought. "I don't know why."

"I suspect she's never attacked you because she's frightened of you."

"Why should Sonia be frightened of me?"

"Because she's frightened of people whom she thinks have succeeded totally in what they paint, write, compose. She's suspicious of anyone who tries to, I think, and, even more, hates the presumption in anyone who tries. She believes, I'm sure, that very, very few people succeed, and that because of the great, the superhuman demands they put on themselves. She thinks most people are pretending. She thinks I'm pretending. And to that I can only say, Well, maybe I am."

He shrugged. "I don't know why she should think I'm not."

I said, "Do you imagine that Sonia has ever wanted to write?"

He was thoughtful again. "Yes, I think she has. I know she was once asked by an editor to do an article, and she was very enthusiastic, but when she submitted it, it was found to be unpublishable. This was a great shock to her. She believed, then, that she didn't have the talent."

"I wonder if her realization that she didn't have talent changed her from the bright, charming, young woman everyone says she was to the dark woman I know her as."

"She lives in terms of others' creativity. She has no illusions about being creative herself."

I said, "I suppose she's simply killed it in herself."

While Sonia was on one of her business trips to London, a mutual friend rang me to say that she was in hospital. He wasn't sure what had happened; she'd been in terrible pain, was taken to hospital, operated on and found to be bleeding internally, but the doctors didn't know what caused the bleeding. However, the friend said, it wasn't grave. Sonia didn't want anyone to visit her in hospital. I realized she would not want anyone to see her suffering, even, perhaps, to know she was suffering.

When, weeks later, she came to dinner, she hardly spoke; she drank two glasses of wine and smoked two cigarettes. She left early.

Then I heard she was in hospital again.

Out of hospital, she moved into a hotel. I rang her there. Her voice sounded alarmingly like that of a little girl. Anxious, I went to the hotel. That little girl's voice told me to come in when I knocked on her door.

She was in bed. She was very thin. In her gaunt, distorted face, the skin around the sockets of her eyes sunk in, her teeth were large and yellow. Shocked, I leaned towards her and kissed her and I sobbed. When I drew back she was smiling; her entire face appeared to be a smile. She suddenly looked very beautiful.

I sat by her bed. I did not know if I should refer to her state, if she'd prefer I didn't; then I thought she of course would have seen it, would have seen it as a fact that had to be accepted for what it was, and I might ask her about her condition as unsentimentally, as matter-of-factly as she had accepted it. I asked, simply, "How are you, Sonia?" "Well," she said, "either I'll survive or I'll die, and though of course we're all faced with either, in my case the either/or will be decided in a very short time. Now tell me about the house in Italy."

I told her stories about the house to make her laugh. When I invited a mutual friend to come stay with me, I told her, he had said, "I think I'll wait till after Sonia's second visit." She laughed, perhaps out of appreciation of my wanting to make her laugh.

Then she said, "I'm very tired."

From Tulsa, I wrote letters to her, one long one about Germaine Greer, who was also at the University of Tulsa.

In early December, in Tulsa, I received a telephone call from London to tell me that Sonia had died that morning. The mutual friend who called was hardly able to speak for weeping. Sonia had bequeathed her organs to the hospital for research; apart from that she had left no instructions as to what was to be done with her body after her death.

I couldn't do anything during the day. In the evening, I went to a friend's for dinner. Germaine was there.

I said, "Sonia died today."

Germaine said nothing. All evening, while I silently listened, she and our friend sang madrigals.

Germaine

THE YEAR SONIA stayed with me in Italy, I did not see Germaine again, after we visited her, until the end of the summer. When I did, she suggested to me that I drive back to London with her. She said, "I'm going to go non-stop, not even to eat. We stop only for petrol and to pee." I had a plane ticket, which I sold for £20.

She said I should close down my stone house and join her in hers on the other side of the mountain for the few days before we left. I waited for her under the pergola of my house, my duffle bag packed; she drove up a road like a rutted dry river bed to collect me, then she drove on similar roads over the mountain.

Her house, long and narrow, with window boxes of white petunias, was high up, in the midst of its beautifully tended garden of all-white flowers. From the garden you looked out over the lower chestnut-covered mountains.

When we arrived we found a baby, about a year and a half old, at a table under the fig tree, playing with finger paints. The baby was slopping green paint on to a shiny piece of wet paper, her hands covered to the wrists; some of the paint was on her face. She was preoccupied and didn't see us until Germaine, standing over her, shouted, "That's not the way to use fucking finger paints," and the baby stared up at her with a look of shocked awe that there was a wrong and a right way to use finger paints.

I went into the house while Germaine taught the baby the use of finger paints. The inside of the house was as beautifully kept as the outside.

The young American mother of the baby was reading a women's magazine.

Germaine shouted to her from outside, "Where the fuck are you while your baby is making a fucking mess out of the fucking finger paints I paid fucking good money for?"

Half smiling at me, the mother dropped her magazine and ran out.

As I didn't know what room I was to have, I waited in the small living room, by the fireplace. I didn't sit. When Germaine came in she looked at me as if I had suddenly appeared in her house, and she seemed about to ask me what I was doing there; she frowned. I smiled. I smiled to remind her who I was, and that I hadn't forced myself into her house, but that she had invited me. I had not even presumed to sit down.

"I'll show you to your room," she said.

The lintels of the doorways were low, and, being tall, she had to bend to go through. I looked at her long legs, long torso, long arms, and her long, curved neck. I followed her through, into her room. It had a large bed, the iron bedstead painted what she called penis pink, and it seemed to me to be the only piece of furniture in the room. She took me through to the next room, my room. Off it was a tiled bathroom.

She laughed. She said, "To get into your room you have to come through mine, and for me to use the bathroom I've got to come through yours."

"That's fine," I said.

"I've put you here intentionally."

Again, I smiled, but more broadly. I didn't ask her what her intention was.

Now, a year or so before, I had been told, severely, by another woman writer, that I was a cunt teaser, and I'd better stop it. I'd not been aware that I was a cunt teaser, and this made me wonder. She said, "You hug women, kiss them, are always pressing against them, and then, of course, you don't follow up in any way on what you make women feel you've promised them." "I don't do that," I said. "You do," she insisted; "study yourself the next time." I hugged her and kissed her, as if on impulse. This writer set her jaw and looked at me closely, then she said she would be able to accept my hugs and kisses, my bodily contact, if I were straightforward; but she thought I was truly duplicitous because I wanted women to imagine me to be a way I wasn't, and this was not only duplicitous, it was perverse. I mustn't do it. I mustn't play with women.

Conscientiously, I stopped.

For all her stature, Germaine was very huggable and kissable.

In my bedroom in her house, it was she who put her arms around me, kissed me at the side of my mouth, and squealed.

I thought: I mustn't cunt tease.

Then she sat on the edge of the bed and said, with a deep sigh, "I don't know what to do with that girl and her baby. I've done everything I can. I invited them out here, paid for everything while they're here, bought special food for the baby, even clothes. You'd think that the least the mother might do is get off her fat ass and watch the child while I'm not here. I'm tired, I'm tired and I'm fed up with taking care of them. I'm always taking care of helpless and hopeless people."

I wanted to do something immediately to show her I was not helpless and hopeless.

I wanted her to think I was quite as efficient as she was.

Before I could think of anything, she got up from the bed and said, "I've been so done in by them, I've become crude. Here, you've just arrived in my house and I haven't even offered you a glass of wine." She sighed again.

We went into the living room, where, on the hearth rug, two sleek white cats had appeared. With a long scooping gesture of both arms, Germaine leaned and took them up, and she buried her face in the fur of one, then the other, saying, "Oh, momma's darlings, momma's beautiful, beautiful darlings." The cats closed their eyes.

I said, "I'll open a bottle of wine for us."

While I opened the bottle, she played with the cats.

"Did you feed them?" she shouted out of the window.

A timid voice responded. "They didn't seem hungry."

"I knew it," Germaine said. "She won't do the fucking simplest thing I ask. She won't even feed the cats. No one ever does the simplest things I ask for, but everyone asks me for the world, the moon, the stars, the whole universe, and my money."

I hoped I conveyed to her by my look that I myself was not asking for anything. Though, perhaps, in some way I was. I felt that I was.

The living room was partly kitchen. Germaine opened the fridge door and looking in said, "What do I have for my darlings? What do I have for my darlings to eat?" She reached inside. The cats had their noses into the bottom of the fridge. "Oh darlings," she said, "you're so lucky. Here's testicle." And she took out, in her hand, a large, yellowish lump with fleshy tissue hanging from it and threw it, with a soft wet thud, on the big wooden chopping block on the table at which I was standing with the open bottle of wine.

"Where're glasses?" I asked.

"In there." She nodded to a cupboard.

As I poured out three glasses of wine she chopped up the testicle with a knife. The cats were mewing at her feet.

I brought a glass of wine out to the American girl, who was sitting quietly by the baby, holding her hand and rubbing one stuck-out finger, green, across the clean sheet of paper. The baby was learning how to use finger paints. Her mother was whispering to her.

Inside again, the cats were eating the chopped-up testicle and Germaine was preparing dinner at the long marble-topped table.

"Is there anything I can do?" I asked.

"You can integrate all the ingredients for a *pesto* sauce in the mortar."

She was frowning, and I wondered what she was thinking. It occurred to me that she might have been thinking: Here I am, again, preparing a meal for guests.

I pounded the wooden pestle into the marble mortar.

At least, I thought, I can be of some help.

The *pesto* reduced to a fine bright green, I said, "I think this is done."

"Let me see," Germaine said, and plunged the pestle up and down. "It's not at all done. It's nowhere near being done. If you're not going to do it properly, why offer to do it? Now I'll do it. I always end up finishing, or putting right, or completely restarting what others do badly. I'll do it."

"Is there anything else I can do?"

"No. I don't think you could. Sit and drink your wine."

From a wicker chair, I watched her pound the pestle. She wore a red dress, and through the knit I could see her bare flesh; her bum, her hips, her tummy, her breasts shook. As I didn't want to disturb her concentration, I was silent. She pounded and pounded, then pushed the mortar aside as if she could no longer bear the look of it. Her hands on her hips, she looked at the table, then about the room, again as if she could hardly bear what she saw; then she looked at me.

"What the fuck are you doing sitting there, drinking wine," she said, "while I'm here doing all the work?"

I smiled, but she didn't smile.

"All right," I said, "you tell me exactly what to do, and I'll do it."

"But you won't do it well."

"I'll try. I really will try."

She didn't tell me what to do, but, an assistant to the chef, I kept order as she, preparing, caused disorder on the table. She accepted my assistance and I was rather pleased with myself.

The mother came in, fed her baby, and put her to bed.

As it got dark, Germaine lit the paraffin lamps.

With everything I ate my sense of taste was brought to fine attention by the fine attention Germaine had given to the food: spaghetti *alla Genovese*, roasted pigeons and small roasted potatoes, salad from the garden, pecorino, grapes.

After dinner, Germaine lit a fire, as an autumn chill was falling.

In my lamp-lit room, naked, I was sitting on the edge of my bed, quietly, when Germaine came in. There was a curtain in the doorway between our rooms which I had not bothered to close. She said, "Oh, I'm sorry," and turned away, but I said, "I don't mind," and she turned back and passed through the room into the bathroom.

She left the door open, and I saw her sitting in the bath, which had burning candles along the edge. Her neck, her shoulders, her breasts shone in the candlelight; she lifted water in her cupped hands to pour it on her, and the splashed water appeared to flame lightly about her.

I remained where I was on the bed, from time to time glancing at her. It was as though I had been living a long time with her, because there was, I felt, a domestic intimacy between us, she in the small bathroom, I in the bedroom off. For the first time I recognized that Germaine could do that: could create a sense of intimacy between herself and another which you'd have thought came only after a long time together, and she did it in a moment, suddenly, and without reference to anything that had recently happened or not happened.

In the still silence the water splashed in her bath.

I got into bed and was all at once very happy, feeling that being with her was and would continue to be all right; I quickly fell asleep, and was unaware of Germaine turning off the paraffin lamp on the little table by my bed.

In the morning I found her, at the table in the living room, doing careful detailed drawings for a dovecot she wanted to build from bricks and roof tiles. To make the drawings, she had proper drafting paper, a proper drafting pen, a ruler, a bottle of india ink.

I said, "It looks as if you're designing a whole palazzo."

"I'm simply doing it the way it should be done," she said.

The mother and the child were playing outside in the sunshine.

I went with Germaine to buy the bricks and tiles. She had two cars, one a battered Cinquecento which she used on the rough, steep part of the road to her house, and, kept parked halfway down on a terrace, a Ford. We got out of the Cinquecento and into the Ford.

As she drove, she thought there was something wrong with the Ford, and she said she wouldn't drive it to London unless she were absolutely sure it was in perfect order. We drove in short, fast bursts, then stopped abruptly. Clouds of dust from the dirt road billowed about us. It was a shock absorber, she said; she was sure it was a shock absorber. She'd take the car to the garage the next day, and if the fault couldn't be found we'd have to fly to London.

I thought: But I've sold my fucking plane ticket.

She said, "I'm not going to risk the lives of that mother and daughter in any way."

The man in the builder's yard didn't have the proper bricks. Germaine talked to him at great length, and I wondered how she knew so much about bricks. She had her drawing, and she discussed it with the man, who because she knew so much about building, took her seriously. She knew, in Italian, all the technical terms.

Afterward, we went to a café at the centre of the small modern town in the plain below the small ancient mountain town. We sat among oleanders flowering in wooden tubs. Germaine said her stomach was upset and ordered Fernet Branca, and as I had never had it I did also. It tasted of the juice of rotted weeds, and I could not imagine how it settled the stomach.

I asked her, "How is it that you know so much about bricks?" She laughed.

Her dress was short, and she was sitting slouched back in her chair, her legs stretched out and open. About her neck she wore an African woman's *cache-sexe* of red and blue beads. I looked from the *cache-sexe* down and saw that she was not wearing underpants and that her cunt was visible. She was looking about at people passing.

I knew she had an Italian lover whom she met often at this café.

She said, "I thought I might see my *gentiluomo* here."

"I've never met him."

"Not that I want to see him," she said. "I don't want to." She laughed. "The last time I saw him here we had a fight and he hit me across the face. One day he'll kill me." She shrugged. "But it doesn't matter. I don't mind if he kills me. I honestly don't."

About her love life, I knew nothing. An article had appeared in an Italian newspaper describing her as a famous women's liber-ationist who lived in a house on a mountainside, from where she telephoned, at whim, men to come up and service her. She was suing the newspaper on the grounds that she had no telephone, and she was, in the Italian court, acting as her own defense. The newspaper wanted to settle out of court, but she refused.

There was a lot of talk among the foreign community about Germaine.

On the way back to the house we stopped in the workshop of a coppersmith, a little man with one tooth and a sweat-stained fedora. In the midst of his shop, Germaine did a drawing for him of what she wanted, a copper hood to go above her fireplace, and he examined it gravely, frowned, spoke, then Germaine spoke, and after a long discussion he agreed to do the job. I did not understand much of what he said, and I didn't understand

Germaine, either; I thought for a moment that her Italian had gone peculiar, until it came to me that she was speaking to him as he spoke, in the local dialect.

Outside, I asked, "But how do you know the dialect?"

"Don't you?" she asked. "You live here. Shouldn't you know the dialect?"

"But I don't know Italian, really. Where did you learn your extraordinary Italian?"

She laughed lightly.

It occurred to me that Germaine did not like to be asked about her life. It was as if she had never learned Italian, but had always known it, not only Italian, but dialects, as she had always known about bricks and copper

Her past I knew nothing of, except that she was Australian and had been to Cambridge.

She said, "I want to get back to the house now. I've got to make sure the baby has had lunch, as well as the mother."

In the afternoon, after a nap, I examined Germaine's library exclusively of women writers, and I sat on the bottom step of the wooden stairs to read one. Germaine, passing from one room into another, came in and said, "I wish I could sit down and read. I wish I could sit down and do some serious writing. I got this place thinking I'd come here and lead a quiet, contemplative life, and out of the contemplation would pour, as out of a great cornucopia, wondrous books. But I haven't written anything here." "Why?" I asked. "I always have people staying and I have to care for them," she said. I said, "You're also always doing something on your house. I don't do anything to my house." She said, going out, "If you have a house, you have to keep it properly. It's a responsibility."

When I went upstairs to my room, Germaine, naked, was in her room, her back to the door. She was against the bright window, and her large body appeared dark. She raised her long arms above her head, then lowered them. The house was quiet, and I thought, in this quiet moment, I shouldn't disturb her to get into my room, and I went back downstairs.

Later, dressed, she came out with a basket and I went down to the kitchen garden with her, on a terrace below the house, where we picked tomatoes which she said she would conserve.

I also picked the remaining aubergines, to make, I said, a special dish for supper, but I wouldn't tell her what it was.

"Then you decide on the menu," she said.

"Oh."

"Tell me what to buy and I'll buy it."

I was taking on a great responsibility.

On the way back to the house we walked along the parterres of white flowers, and Germaine from time to time would lean low over the beds and shout out, "Come on, you fucking flowers, come on! Bloom, bloom!"

While Germaine was out in the late afternoon, after five o'clock when the shops reopened for the day, I started to prepare the dish. This required building a fire in the fireplace and reducing the blaze to embers; but the fire kept going out, and when it caught, a little, it smoked into my face. Germaine came back to find me still trying to get a fire reduced to embers. She said, "You're doing it like a fucking fairy. Let me do it." "Like a what?" I asked. She made a face. Within fifteen minutes she had knocked the fire down to bright hot embers.

"What shall I do?" she asked.

"Well, you can make the lamb stew."

"What kind of stew?"

"In a tomato sauce."

Between then and supper I prepared only one dish, which required grilling the aubergines over the embers till their skins were charcoal black, scraping out the insides, squeezing the bitter juices out and mixing the pulp with butter and milk, salt and lots of pepper.

Germaine had invited an elderly American friend up from the valley for supper. He said about the dish I'd prepared, which, in combination with the stew, was called, approximately, *hueji-abendi*,. "This really is different from anything I've ever had." Germaine ate without expression, as if she wouldn't recognize that the aubergine dish was in any way special. But I knew it was special.

She had prepared everything else.

I said, "The stew is really delicious."

She could not give a compliment, I saw, and she could not accept a compliment; she remained expressionless, her mouth pulled down so her nostrils, too, were pulled down, and her face was longer than usual.

Even while sitting at the table, Germaine seemed to be doing something other than sitting at the table and eating, and that other was more important; and if she could not in fact be doing that other, she was actively thinking about it. I recognized that she was always doing something other in her mind, and as intense as her concentration was in what she was doing, there was an air about her of considering, more intensely, something else. I had the vivid impression from her of, at some high level, trying to sort out, not her personal problems, but other people's problems.

Most of Germaine's talk at dinner was about infibulation, female circumcision, among tribes in Africa. She described how older women performed the operation on younger, using, at best, rusty razor blades. In severe cases, the clitoris was cut out and the inner lips of the labia; what was, in fact, a bloody wound was bound shut with grass tied tightly about the thighs, a straw inserted to insure an orifice large enough for urine and menstrual discharge to pass, and the wound was allowed to heal. When the time came for the woman to give herself to her new husband, he cut her open and fucked her; then a wooden copy of his erect cock was placed in the wound, and she was bound again, so only her husband, he thought, had access to her. As men with the same size, and smaller, cocks had access to her also, Germaine said a man who wanted to keep his wife his only should naturally want to have a very small cock. Of course, the woman, whose genitals were scar tissue, did not care much if she was fucked or not. Each time she gave birth, she had to be cut open.

Often as she spoke I put my hands between my legs and held my genitals.

After the American left and the mother joined her baby, Germaine and I drank wine and talked.

She said, "All evening I've been thinking about that mother and her baby and what can be done for them."

The next day Germaine was very active, at the house and away. Sometimes she went off alone, sometimes I went with her. I recall the results of her activity in final images: many jars of conserved tomatoes, a miniature loden coat for the little girl—

In the garage where I went with her to have the car checked, she talked to two mechanics with grease-stained arms and Tuscan golden eyes, and as she spoke to them she appeared to dance lightly about the garage, among the dismantled cars and car parts. They stared at her. Perhaps they had never known a woman who could swing her hips from side to side and clasp her hands to her breasts and pucker her mouth and know as much as they did about shock absorbers.

They, as did all the locals, called her La Dottoressa.

By the time we were ready to leave—the big Ford packed, a basket of *panini* with ham, of cheese, of fruit, and a bottle of brandy at my feet by Germaine in the front seat, and a bed made in the back for the baby—the sun was setting.

Germaine said, "This is going to be one fucking bad trip. I wish I were going back to London by plane."

As we passed Cortona, the town, high on the side of a mountain among olive trees and cypresses, was still in sunlight, and beaming.

"We have a rule," Germaine said; "no one ever points to anything and says, 'Look at that, how beautiful it is.'"

In the plain, passing a field of the stumps of sunflowers, I said, "Look at that, how ugly it is."

It was soon dark. The baby fell asleep, as did the mother in the back seat. Germaine drove up into northern Italy, towards the Brenner Pass. She drove very fast, so the highway lights seemed to stream about the car.

The night itself became a country, floating above the other countries, which was measured not in terms of hours, but kilometres; the night was hundreds of kilometres long. Though we stopped for passport control at the Austrian and German borders, the real frontier, I felt, was when we crossed from darkness into dawn.

All night, Germaine talked, or so I imagine now she did. What I most recall was her telling me about her sexual experiences. As often happened after I listened to Germaine talk, I recall vivid images, and the most vivid is this: a dark, thin, intense Italian used-car salesman took her to the sea outside Melbourne one summer evening, at hot, green sunset, where, lying on the beach, people were sleeping wrapped completely in white sheets; there was a sharp, hot wind, and the sheets thrashed about the still bodies, among which Germaine followed the used-car salesman down to the sea, deep green; he took her hand and led her into the sea, both of them clothed, so she felt the rising and falling water pull at her clothes, and, in the waves, he fucked her.

As Germaine told me such stories, I felt that I was being taken into her confidence, into her private world; that is, I was taken into the private world of a public woman, where I learned something about her no one else knew. But I also felt that she was not talking to me, but to anyone, and what I heard anyone could hear.

Her only secret was this: she would not reveal how she had become Germaine Greer, how she had learned everything she had had to learn to become the person she was. She would reveal everything about the Germaine Greer who actually was, who was entirely public, and about whom she kept no secrets.

As for her sexual activities, they were not dark and private, but activities in which the world was engaged and which were in large part determined by, and with study might explain something of, the world she lived in. She talked about those various activities (she preferred men for their bit of gristle) as if talking about the sexual activities of the outside world.

At a petrol station in Germany we all got out to pee. It was dark and cold. Back in the car, I waited with the mother and the woken baby for Germaine, who was, I thought, taking a long time. She came, finally, with a silver envelope containing a condom, which she had bought from a machine. I wondered if she had gone into the men's room for it, or if there was a dispensing machine in the ladies'. She was interested in it, she said, because it was advertised as prolonging love-making. Before she started the car, she tore open the envelope and pulled out the condom and stuck a finger in it. "Just as I thought," she said. "It's coated inside with a lubricant which simply numbs the cock." A bit of evidence for some scientific research on contraception, I thought. She threw it and the envelope out.

We drove off. It began to rain. Germaine took long pulls from the bottle of brandy. We played word games. It rained harder, then stopped.

With dawn, we went into the country of light, a light rising from the flat wet green-grey countryside like a mist. The autobahn was deserted. The first sign I saw in the daylight was DACHAU. Germaine went silent.

A long time afterward I said, "Look, another sign for Ausfahrt. What a funny name for a town."

For the first time since Dachau, she spoke, laughing. "You nit, that means exit."

We were silent again.

She said, "Another sign for Ausfahrt. All roads in Germany lead to Ausfahrt."

After a prolonged silence, driving very fast, she began to talk quietly to her car, sometimes patting the dashboard.

"You're doing well, baby. You're doing so well, my baby."

Whenever we stopped for petrol, Germaine, I thought, spoke, not simply German, but the German of the region. She might even say, afterward, that the garage man who'd served us wasn't from the area, but, according to his accent, from another region.

By ten in the morning we were in Belgium, a country, she said, of no shadows.

The mother and the baby woke. The baby had to pee, which she did, as before, in a pot her mother held for her. The pot was handed to me; I rolled down the window, stuck the pot far out, tipped it upside down, and the pee was sprayed back in through the window, into our faces. Pee was dripping from Germaine's nose. She laughed. I looked at the mother and the baby; the mother, too, was laughing lightly, wiping her face with her fingers, but the baby, her pee dripping from her face, looked shocked. Perhaps she wasn't sure if this was meant to happen or not. Perhaps, in the month away, she had had a lot of shocks.

At Ostend we waited in the car in a queue for the ferry. Germaine took out a little round mirror to look at herself, holding the mirror at different angles. Then she put on some makeup and combed out her hair; she combed it out till it stood on end.

We had a late lunch on the ferry. The American girl said something I didn't hear, as it was said in a low voice; it made

Germaine explode, and the explosion made her hair stand out more.

She said, "You and your child can just get out of my sight for a while."

The mother and the baby went off to walk about the deck.

Germaine ordered drinks, vodka and tomato juice.

I said, "I'll bet there've been a lot of people in your life whom you've taken on to help, and whom you've resented helping."

She looked at me, her eyes narrow. "You think I ask for it, do you?"

"Well, no relationship is one-sided. If she's with you for you, you're with her for some reason, too."

Her face twisted, and a shock seemed to make her hair vibrate. "I wanted to help."

A little boy, half tripping, came running into the restaurant, followed by the American girl's child, who ran after him.

In a loud voice, Germaine said, "I know what you're after, baby. You want to give him a blow job."

The little boy went out, and the little girl, toddling, went after him.

Germaine sighed.

The mother came through, looking for her daughter.

Germaine sighed again.

At Dover, Germaine said, "Here we are in the country of the grey underpants."

I began to hallucinate, seeing, in the gathering twilight, buildings from other countries. I wondered if, after more than twenty-four hours of driving, Germaine too might be hallucinating; then I imagined that she wouldn't hallucinate, that her strong will would keep her seeing only what was there, the dual carriageway, the lights, the signs. Her face was tense with concentration. Her hair was electric in the way it stood out. I depended on her, on the clarity and power of her concentration, to get me through my hallucinations to London.

After she left off her friend and the baby, she came to my flat, where we had scrambled eggs. If she gave in to being tired, it was by talking more and more about the mother and baby. I wondered if she were hallucinating about them. Abruptly, she stood to go to her house.

She said, "I want, I need, someone to sleep with tonight."

I kissed her good night.

Over the following days, I thought a lot about Germaine, and my thinking made of her a large public woman obsessed with the world, the entire world; she was difficult towards people in the world because so few cared a fuck about it.

When, a week later, she came to dinner, I asked her about the mother and the baby; she said, "They're staying with me again." She sighed. "Well, what's to be done for such people? What?"

2

IN THE LATE summer of 1980, I was in New York, on my way to Oklahoma, where I was to be writer in residence for the autumn term at the University of Tulsa. Germaine was also to be there, as she'd been the previous autumn term, setting up the Tulsa Center for the Study of Women's Literature. I had seen her in Italy the summer before, and she'd said to me about Tulsa, "The people there are good people. You'll be treated very well. But you're not going to find many men of a particular sex in Tulsa, Oklahoma." I said, "What sex is that?" She drew in her chin and pursed her lips; she put her hands to her breasts and threw out a hip and fluttered her eyelashes. She said, "If you don't know, my dear, you can't expect me to tell you." I laughed. In New York, I could not imagine Tulsa inhabited by any people, of no matter what sex, except for Germaine.

I was staying with a friend on the West Side; invited one hot Sunday afternoon to lunch by another friend on the East Side, I walked through Central Park. I tried to keep my course across the park by sighting a tall pointed building on the East Side, but, among narrow paths about hillocks and mulberry woods and scummy ponds, I got lost; I walked round and round, and came out of the woods into a meadow; in the high, dry grass of the meadow were hundreds of men, all in narrow bathing trunks, sun bathing, and as I walked along the path at the edge of the meadow they moved, as if together, and looked at me. Their oiled bodies gleamed. I walked quickly, though it was hot and dusty.

The path took me through woods again, then out on to a wide flat playing field, and I sighted my tall pointed building.

As I walked, slowly, I thought of what Germaine had said.

I could not imagine myself among those men, in their country. It frightened me, I knew, because there were no women in it.

This occurred to me in Central Park: why should I, who was supposed to be independent of women, so want to be with women?

When, after I returned to the West Side, I told this to my friend, he said, laughing, "Not just women—difficult women."

"Oh Christ," I said.

Why, I thought, why was I so anticipating being in Tulsa with Germaine, whom I knew to be an enormously difficult woman?

I arrived a few days before she did, and stayed with the Dean. With him I went to meet Germaine at her hotel. It was white-hot in Oklahoma, and all surfaces seemed to vibrate in the heat. In the cool car I kept asking myself why I was anxious about seeing her, as if my stay in Tulsa were not going to be judged by the University, the graduate department, my students, but Germaine. For some reason, my success or failure seemed to depend on her. I was talking with the Dean about Tulsa and thinking, at the same time, about Germaine. Then I thought: You must sort this out. We drove under the portico of the big, glassy, modern hotel, and there she was, waiting outside the revolving glass doors, her shoes held by their straps in her hand. I got out to meet her, and kissed her, lightly, on both cheeks.

"Isn't it extraordinary," I said, "that we should have seen one another last in Cortona, Italy, and this time in Tulsa, Oklahoma?"

She scowled a little. "I don't think it's at all extraordinary."

As she walked barefoot across the pavement, I looked down at her feet. It was the first time I had noticed that they were broad and stubby. I had, before, thought of her as beautiful beyond any fault. I had thought of her, large, standing high above me and looking down upon me, a very beautiful public woman. Her feet made her, in one small part, a private women. But she was private only in her feet. At the car, she put her shoes on.

I sat in the back seat. By the Dean in the front, she said, "For all that it's supposed to be the best hotel in Tulsa, it's fucking awful. I rang room service for a bottle of champagne, and they had nothing but Californian, no French. What a fucking provincial place I've come to."

The Dean said, "Some of those California champagnes can be pretty good."

"Pretty good is not good enough."

We joined the Dean's wife and children at a Chinese restaurant. Germaine's talk had nothing to do with where she had been or what she'd done since she was last in Tulsa; what she talked about was contraception and abortion, and we, silent at the round table, listened; she opened up about us the great problems of contraception and abortion around the round world. She was obsessed with the whole world and what was happening, or not happening, in it. We were among peasant women in India, aboriginal women of Australia, middle-class women of northern Italy, and Germaine was concerned for them all, and angry that so few others were concerned. She seemed not to be very much aware of us, who were attentive to the details of her stories: infanticide as practiced by women in certain cultures by smothering the baby in ash, or throwing it against a tree, or placing a stick across the throat and standing on both ends. As well as anger, there was a look of grief and pain on Germaine's face. We were all silent for a while. "What's to be done?" she asked. "About unwanted children, what's to be done?"

When we got out of the restaurant the after-sunset sky was green and mauve, and huge, and strung out low against it were black poles and cables. I was in a country I had never been in before.

I said, "Look at that. Look."

The Dean said, "It's the big sky of the West."

Germaine said nothing. I wondered if she lived, not in the particular country in which she was bodily, but in the general, problematic world which obsessed her. And then it came to me: Germaine's awareness of the world was totally unliterary.

We had our offices in a small brick house on campus. The house was isolated in a great black space of parking lots, surrounded by stumps of trees which had been cut down because of disease. In half the house Germaine was setting up the Women's Literature Center, and at the back of the house I had my office; between us was a kitchen.

I went at odd hours to my office, and every time I went I found Germaine, often alone, in the Center, working. She had filled the fridge in the kitchen with beer and fruit juices, and we drank and talked a little there.

Alone with her, I felt that she was disapproving of me in a way I couldn't understand, and I told myself she was often and arbitrarily disapproving of people. We talked about Italy and England, not about ourselves, and she was abrupt.

Then one late afternoon she said, frowning, "You told friends in Italy that I'm a castrating woman."

"Well, you are," I said.

I saw her frown deepen.

"But you may like to know that's not the reason why I've been looking forward to being here with you."

She grunted a little. She said, "Would you like to have supper together?"

I thought: If she's been offended by what I said privately about her months before, how offended must she be by what is said against her publicly day after day?

At supper in one of Tulsa's fancy restaurants, I asked her questions about contraception and abortion, which she answered with vivid anecdotes; and I asked her questions about female sexuality, and what a woman felt during orgasm, and, again, she was vivid, and to help me understand used similes: her own long, long, violently fluttering orgasms were like . . . She talked and talked about women and sex. It occurred to me that I listened as though I had never heard anything about the subject.

One white-hot Sunday afternoon early in the term I arrived at my office to find Germaine, with a male friend, painting the walls of the Center a bright red, Liberty Red. She had decided to do it herself, even to buying the paint, rather than have Maintenance do it, because she said, they wouldn't do it for weeks, and they'd do it badly. The furniture in the two rooms was pushed to the middle, and on a long, drop-cloth-covered table, among cans of red paint, were paper plates of fried chicken and an ice-filled cooler with champagne bottles sticking out. Standing on a chair, Germaine's friend, his shirt tails out and sweating, was painting a corner, and Germaine, in a dress, was painting low on a wall. She didn't crouch, but bent her long body at the waist to reach down and painted with long, loose strokes.

"I'll help," I said.

"Have a glass of champagne first," Germaine said.

It was pleasant inside, with the air-conditioners going and the champagne and chicken. I felt I had come into a centre of privileged pleasure.

"I'll get my clothes covered in paint," I said, "so I'd better take them off."

Maybe it was partly because Germaine wore no under-clothes—sometimes, if she had on a dress that buttoned down the front, when she sat the space between the buttons would gape open and you saw her pubic hair—that her bodily presence was always so powerful. With Germaine's own body in mind, I undressed to my narrow briefs, and even took off my shoes and socks. Just arrived from Italy, I was tanned, and work with the peasants in the valley had, I thought, tightened me up. So, aware of Germaine's body, I was aware of my own.

Brush dripping red paint, I strutted about.

"What do you want me to do?" I asked.

"The little areas we missed," she said.

As I painted, she came up to me, put her hand on my behind, and said, "I like a nice ass."

This made me happy. Her touching me was not only an acceptance, but a justification of my body by a woman who had the authority to justify anything.

We drank champagne, she, her friend, I. I was not sure if she and the other man were lovers. I didn't care. We continued to paint, and, at moments, laughing, one hand with the red brush held up, I embraced and kissed her, and she responded by embracing and kissing me at other moments.

Whenever his back was turned, Germaine stuck out her tongue at her friend.

After we finished the painting of the two rooms—which

Germaine called the right and left ventricles of the Liberty Red heart of the Center—the three of us went to a fish restaurant on the North Side of Tulsa.

In a booth next to a wide window (outside was the parking lot with trucks and big cars, and, beyond, low brick buildings with billboards on them, and above and beyond that the hot, bright sky), we ate fried oysters and scallops and catfish and corn balls and drank cold beer. To me, everything was an object of a new, vast awareness; I commented on everything in the restaurant, which her friend, from Tulsa, of course took for granted, but Germaine smiled, and I thought, She approves of my enthusiasm, and that made me more enthusiastic.

"Look at that!" she said.

I turned. Into the restaurant had come a black man wearing a short-sleeved shirt, loose, which was a patchwork of reproductions of Matisse paintings. He wore, in miniature: *Grand intérieur rouge, Le rêve, Grande robe bleue fond noir, L'escargot, Jeune fille en jaune, La leçon du piano, Madame Matisse, Les plumes blanches, Baigneuses, Les marocains.*

I said to Germaine, "What does that mean? What, that a black man in a fish restaurant in Tulsa, Oklahoma, should be wearing a whole museum full of Matisse's greatest paintings?"

She raised her eyebrows and kept looking at the man.

On the way out, she went to his booth and asked him where he had got the shirt, as she wanted one also.

Her friend drove us back to the little brick house on campus and left us off. She and I had more champagne, and she talked about the friend.

She said, "I invited him to Italy this past summer, but he didn't notice anything, anything. It was as if nothing he saw, heard, tasted, smelled, or felt, was in any way different from anything he'd seen, heard, tasted, smelled, felt here in Tulsa. He was unaware, totally and blankly unaware. I couldn't bear it. I can't bear unawareness. I can't. It takes so little, so little, to *see*—"

"Yes, yes," I said.

"To *see* the sky over fucking Tulsa, Oklahoma, if you're not utterly blind."

It occurred to me that she was referring to my enthusiasm for the skyscape the first evening we were together here. I'd remarked on the huge green and mauve sky and the telephone poles because I'd wanted her to know that I was aware, when she seemed to me to be unaware. But she was aware.

She was always aware.

Our classes began. Germaine had a Monday evening seminar at the Center, and every Monday afternoon she prepared, in the kitchen between our offices, soup for her students. She bought big cooking pots, bowls, spoons, a ladle, a chopping board.

She said, "This seminar lasts three hours. My students need some food to get them through. Then, I think I should open their taste buds as much as the buds of their tender little brains."

Each week, she prepared a different soup: gazpacho, avocado soup, cucumber and yoghurt—

From my office, in the evening, I heard her conducting the seminar. She read out passages of poetry in different dramatic voices, and she sometimes shouted, "Listen! Listen! Use your ears!"

On the red walls of the Center she had hung reproductions of paintings by women and a large plan on which, down one side, were listed the eighteenth-century women writers her students were reading—Mary Chudleigh, Mary Leapor, Mary Molesworth Monck, Mary Masters, Mary Wortley Montagu—and, down the other side, the important contemporary historical events. More and more women writers were added over the weeks.

When I went into my office in the morning, I sometimes found objects missing—a bulletin board, a typewriter stand on wheels—which had been appropriated by Germaine for the Center. She said, "You didn't need them. We need them."

Sometimes I found a gift from her on my desk: a bottle of retsina, a book she had bought for me—

Some of her students were in my workshop. They called me by my given name; she insisted on being called Dr Greer.

She said, "They've got to fucking well bear in mind that, for the time being, I know more than they do."

There was a third office in the little brick house, occupied by a mutual friend in charge of university publications. Whenever

Germaine was away giving a lecture I found myself talking about her to this friend, obsessively.

Over and over, I said, "Germaine is an entirely public woman. You can't presume to be intimate with her. Even in private, she's public."

"What do you mean?"

"I'm convinced she's interested only in public issues, not personal issues. You know, I don't think Germaine really has friends, close friends, and I think she doesn't because she's not interested in her relationships, she's not interested in herself. She's only interested in other people, and that, somehow, depersonalizes her interest. Does this make any sense?"

"I'll have to think about it," our friend said.

"So will I," I said.

Germaine was devoted to her Center and the students in it as if to the one world she might make work properly; she arrived early in the morning and left late at night, and while she was there telephones rang all the time, typewriters clacked, papers appeared to fly about, and she, exuding the scent of patchouli, kept it all going. If I met one of our students in the kitchen, we talked a bit; Germaine, hearing us, would shout, "Come on, come on, there's work to do," and the student would run back. She expected them to be as devoted to the Center as she was. The scent of her patchouli was always present, even when she was away; but when she was away there was an air of quiet withdrawal among the students.

She said, "What they've got to learn, more than anything, is that there is a world outside them which demands as much attention, if not more, than their sad, introverted selves."

Yet she quickly learned everything about their private lives, and talked to me, with worried concern, about one who was divorcing her husband, another who had just got out of the Navy in which he'd had some unbalancing experiences, another who hadn't had a period in six months, another whose grandfather had died and to whom, because he couldn't afford it, Germaine had given money for the plane fare to the funeral and back, another who had an unwanted pregnancy. At the back of the Center, she had a little office of her own; the door was often closed, and I knew she was having private conferences with students.

Later, she'd say, "What can be done for——?", and sigh.

I arrived one day to find the Center filled with cameras, lights, silver reflecting umbrellas, and, in the midst, Germaine being interviewed about her work there by a woman with a spiral notebook and pencil.

Every Thursday, just before a class she was giving on Byron, Keats and Shelley, we had, the two of us alone, lunch in a Greek restaurant, and we talked about England and Italy.

Though I told myself I could live anywhere, Tulsa struck me, in all its particulars, as very strange, and I was never sure where I stood in relation to the particulars. In a supermarket, I would suddenly become unsure of what I should buy, and I had to think about whatever I was doing. When in a supermarket with Germaine, however, I noticed she went from shelf to shelf, pushing the shopping cart, as if she had been there all her life.

After two weeks, she was speaking with a Tulsan accent.

I liked to be with Germaine because she was, in her freedom to say and do anything, anywhere, always unpredictable in her reactions—her reactions to the world around us, and her reactions to me and what I said and did. Though this frightened me, in that I ran the constant risk of saying or doing the wrong thing, I was excited. It was when I was alone with her that I was most excited. And even though I was alone with her I felt that the risk I ran could be seen, at any moment, by the whole world. Private risks were, with her, very public. It amused me when, at our formica-topped table, eating our pasticcio, she might suddenly say in a loud voice, "How fucking wonderful," and the Tulsans in the restaurant turned to look. She might as easily, as far as I knew her, have shouted, "How fucking awful."

Every Thursday, she ate with her fingers half of the pickled chillis in a bottle on the table.

We were often invited together to drinks or dinner parties, and there we found ourselves talking to one another.

At dinner with six others, Germaine said to me across the dinner table, "I haven't had sex in weeks, not since I got here." "Neither have I," I said. She said, "Well, I've been happy enough in my little white room taking care of it all by myself." "I'm pretty content in that way, too," I said.

Most often we went to parties together; she would pick me up in her car because I didn't know my way around Tulsa. When I went alone I'd find her talking usually to no less than three other people.

Because I'd thought she didn't want to talk about her past, as if she had decided that her past simply didn't matter to her as she was now, I'd never tried to learn about it. I arrived at a party one evening to find her, in a large armchair, describing, to a full room, her family. This was startling. I sat among the others and listened.

I thought: Perhaps she can only be so intimate about herself in a public way.

Then I noted that she would, to people she didn't at all know and would most probably never see again, reveal what many people would reserve for a close friend. She might, in talking, suddenly observe about herself: "I can't show affection. When a lover meets me at an airport, I go rigid and ask him if he got the plumber in or had the car repaired. I don't know why. I can't do it." Or: "As much as I like fucking, I don't like sleeping the night with someone I've fucked with. I usually end up sleeping on the floor beside the bed."

I also remarked that, in talking to people she didn't know, she might make an aside which would indicate worlds of experience she had had about which I, who imagined I knew her, had heard nothing. She'd say, "When I took care of mentally retarded children." Or: "When I sang in the Bach B Minor Mass." Or: "When I was a waitress." The many lives she seemed to have had, revealed in flashes by such comments, revolved one within the other within the other. "When I worked with fishermen in Calabria." "When I acted." "When I . . ." She was stating her credentials for making an observation about the care of mentally retarded children, or Bach, or waitressing.

A colleague said to me, "Isn't there anything she doesn't know about from her own experience?"

Late one weekend evening she rang me from her office. Her voice was high. "*Non ne posso più*. Will you come and fetch me, and take me to a restaurant, and let me talk?"

I dressed in my summer suit, as it was still hot in Oklahoma, and drove my rented car to the campus and the brick house, whose lights, alone of all the university buildings, were lit and beaming out on to the empty, dark parking lot. Her having rung gave me, I realized, a strange confidence, which I interpret retrospectively and which that evening I was full of: Germaine's widening acceptance of me.

She was in a white dress which swung loosely with the movements of her body.

At the restaurant, we started with a bottle of champagne.

She talked on and on, with developing obsession, developing, I thought, to a point at which her higher and higher pitched voice would break, about the Center.

"I'm running it myself," she said. "It's important. God damn it. It is important."

"You must make everyone know how important," I said.

She leaned towards me and in a lowered voice said, "Do you realize you're the only person here I understand?"

She hadn't said, "the only person here who understands me", but, "the only person I understand", and with this I felt a sudden pleased wonder at what there was to understand about me.

I imagined she had a structured vision of me, and she might, if I asked her, articulate it. She had the intelligence to.

I said, "And you're the only person here I understand."

I was always vividly aware of Germaine as a woman, a large, imposing woman. Her intelligence was to me the intelligence of a woman, because she had, as a woman, thought out her role in the world; the complexity of the role required intelligence to see it, and she had seen it, I thought, thoroughly. Even when, once, she said to me, "I don't understand women at all," I took this as an observation of what it was to be a woman. So, if I with some degree of logic believed Germaine understood me, it followed that I believed she understood me with a woman's intelligence. I wanted to know what she understood.

I was drunk on champagne.

I wanted her to tell me what she thought about me. I believed I needed her to tell me. She stared at me. I stared back.

I didn't say anything.

She continued to talk about the Center.

Going to bed, I thought: A relationship with a woman did this for me: it made me feel complicated.

We often had dinner together in different restaurants.

As most restaurants were closed, late one evening, she said we'd drive out of Tulsa to a Mexican place where the guacamole was a whole meal. She drove fast, and faster, in bursts, over empty stretches of highway out of Tulsa, shouting out. Rounding an unlit curve, I saw ahead in the headlights a black and white wooden barrier with red lights flashing on it; Germaine swerved to miss it, and, the tires screeching, the car turned into a crossing where a lone bicyclist was pedalling; she swerved again, so the car missed the bicyclist, who simply looked back at us and continued to pedal, and we stopped across the highway.

"Are you all right?" she asked.

"Yes."

"Why the fuck weren't there any signs warning us that there'd be a barrier round the curve?" She was very angry. "I would have slowed down and we wouldn't have had this *scemenza*." Frowning, she righted the car and we drove to the restaurant.

As we ate the guacamole, her anger left her, and she kept repeating, "I really should have been more careful. I really should have."

"There should have been signs before the curve," I said.

"No, no, it was my fault. I wasn't careful. I drove badly." She hunched her shoulders up, put a hand across her mouth, and looked at me with the look of a deeply embarrassed girl. Through her hand, she said, "I drove very badly. I shouldn't have done that. I'm very sorry."

"I felt you were in control."

"It shouldn't have happened, and wouldn't have if I'd been driving properly." She placed her other hand over the first, across her mouth, and she hunched her shoulders closer together. "Oh dear."

I had never before seen her embarrassed; and she was because she had performed badly.

At the Graduate School of Letters staff meetings, I understood little because I was unfamiliar with academic jargon. Germaine knew the jargon, and hearing her discuss a certain problem it came to me why everyone listened to her with such attention: she had a command of whatever vocabulary happened to be appropriate to the problem. She was the only woman at the meetings.

One morning, I sat in the large leather swivel chair at the large polished desk in my office, which I kept stark and empty. (Germaine had made her own private office at the back of the Center personal with paintings of and by women, a kelim thrown over a sofa, her own books in the book shelves.) I looked to the side of my room, where there should have been a high-backed leather chair, and in its stead I saw a small, rickety, paint-spattered chair. I jumped up, ran through the kitchen into the Center, and shouted, "Where is my chair?" Germaine was out. Her assistants, some of whom were my students, looked for the chair, which was in Germaine's office.

"I'm very angry," I said.

I exchanged the chairs.

Later that day I encountered Germaine in the kitchen, making soup.

"You took my chair," I said.

"I deserved it," she said.

"No you didn't. I deserve it. And, anyway, it's mine."

"I deserve it," she said, "and I should have it."

"Well, you're not going to get it."

Smiling, I went back into my office.

In a loud voice, I heard Germaine say, "We need more room for the Center. We need more office space."

I went out. "You're not getting my office," I said.

"We need it," she said.

"You're not going to get it."

She stuck out her tongue at me.

I said, "You know all the tricks of expansionist politics."

"How else can I get what I have to get?" she said.

I said, "I'm going to make it a condition of my staying here that I keep this office."

I thought: That's what she would do.

With her, I was always conscious of trying to speak at least grammatically, and sometimes with style. She said I had a peculiar accent, but she never corrected me, as she sometimes corrected others, especially, of course, her students. Once I said, "I still feel disorientated here." She said, "Disoriented." "No," I said, "it's 'disorientated'." "No, it isn't." "It is." "I know it isn't." I said, "It is." I looked it up in the *OED*, and found both words; but, strictly, "disorient" was defined as "to cause to lose one's bearings", and "disorientate" as "to turn from an eastward position". The next time I saw Germaine I told her that I'd looked up the word in the *OED* and that I was right, though I was wrong. She simply pursed her lips. When I was alone with our friend I told her what I had done, and she said, "Just a while ago I said 'disoriented' to Germaine, and she corrected me and said, no, it was 'disorientated'." I said, "She took my word."

A week before Thanksgiving, I had a party at my house for some of my students. I also invited a drag queen I had met in Tulsa. Germaine, too.

In the kitchen, I found Germaine talking animatedly to the drag queen. I stood by them and listened. Germaine took on the gestures and the accent of the young queen, a thin boy, as if she herself were a drag queen, or at least knew everything there was to know about being one, and she was talking to the queen, named Dou Dou, as an equal. They were talking about street trade.

After the party, I said to Germaine, "You were getting on very well with that drag queen."

She said, "She was brave."

I felt in the very presence of Germaine's body the positive power of some kind of political sex. She herself meant something in the world, and any relationship with her had to be meaningful in the world. In the same way that she saw the most intimate of intercourses, sex, as meaningful in the world, a relationship with her had to be political, had to do with the world outside.

3

GERMAINE WAS LOOKING drawn and pale. On one of our Thursdays at lunch in the Greek restaurant (she was beginning to speak a little Greek to the owners) we decided to go away together for the Thanksgiving break.

I said, "You really need a rest. If we go anywhere, it must be to a place where you can rest properly."

Her eyes large, she looked at me as if to say: Do you imagine that I don't know that?

With Germaine, there was always the fear of stating the obvious.

We planned on going to Santa Fé, New Mexico, where neither of us had been.

We left directly after Germaine's last class before the holiday break. It was a cold, grey afternoon. We were told it would snow and we might not be able to make it across the Texas panhandle. One of our students gave us votive candles in case we got stuck in the snow, though I wasn't quite sure what we were supposed to do with them; another gave us a flashlight. Packing Germaine's car with our bags, a huge electric typewriter, piles of books about gardens, I had a sense that we were going very far. A few of our students waved us off from the little brick house.

Germaine insisted on driving because, she said, I drove too slowly.

On the back seat of the car was a Styrofoam cooler, without ice, and in it three bottles of champagne. Before we got out of Tulsa, we stopped at a grocery store to buy a big bag of ice for the cooler. Germaine also bought four or five clear plastic bags of liquorice.

As soon as we got back into the car she said, "Open a bag of liquorice, will you, and give me three sticks together." Her eyes narrowed on the highway, she held out her hand and I placed the liquorice in it. She ate the three sticks together. "More," she said, and again she held out her hand.

"You really like liquorice," I said.

"It's good for my hernia," she said.

I wondered where she had heard that liquorice is good for hernia. Then I thought: Germaine wouldn't have heard it from anyone, but would always have known that liquorice is good for hernia.

I kept giving her liquorice sticks whenever she held out her hand. Her eyes were always on the road, as she was driving fast. She read out loud all the highway signs. And she was on the lookout for police cars. She said she was lucky with the police; they only appeared when she happened to be going slowly. As we slowed down to turn off one highway on to another, a police car approached us from the opposite lane. "You see?" she said. She held out her hand for more liquorice.

When we crossed over into the Texas panhandle she shouted out, "Whoopee," and hit her thigh. "Open a bottle of champagne," she said.

The champagne foamed in and spilled over our plastic cups. The sky was low over the low, snow-covered land, in which, at great distances, were oil pumps and drilling derricks. As we drank the champagne the sky darkened.

Our first stop in Texas was at Shamrock, where we pulled up at the Blarney Stone Inn, just off the highway. To have a beer, because we were in a dry county, I had to join a club. We ordered T-bone steaks and baked potatoes; the steaks had to mushy excess the one quality which Germaine said Americans demand in their meat: that you should be able to gum them. The Blarney Stone Inn appeared, as all buildings in that part of America seemed to me, to have been put up temporarily; I was aware that beyond the walls of the dining room was the vast outside. Inside it was empty except for Germaine and me, a fat waitress at a table next to the kitchen smoking a cigarette, and, at the other side of the room from us, an old, skeletal couple, also eating soft steaks and baked potatoes.

The woman had short, dyed red hair. He was in a check jacket and differently checked trousers. She called to the waitress for a doggie bag; when she took the bag the fat waitress handed her, she said, "This isn't a doggie bag. A doggie bag is lined with plastic so it won't drip. This is just an ordinary old paper bag." The waitress didn't answer, but slumped off. The old woman said to the old man, "But this isn't a doggie bag."

As we ate, Germaine and I studied the couple as if we were trying, through them, to understand a little the place we were in. Sometimes Germaine stopped eating to look at them.

Beyond them was the bar; through an open double doorway we saw men in brim-rolled stetsons and boots drinking and smoking. In the bar was a juke box and a small dance floor, which the old couple, he pulling her chair out from the table and taking her arm to lead her, went to; the old lady put a coin in the juke box and chose some records, loud rock music, and she and the man, stiffly swinging their arms and barely lifting their feet, danced. Sometimes she stepped back from him and clapped her hands and said, "Yeah, yeah, yeah," while he, alone, shuffled his feet back and forth and moved his arms in startling jerks.

As we left, by way of the smoky bar, I heard the old woman say to the old man, over the music, "If this place can't give you a real doggie bag, it must be a dump."

We went on to Amarillo. The snow on the ground deepened as we went west, and the roads became icy. Germaine drove with great care, slowing down when she saw ahead parts of the highway where there was bound to be ice: under an overpass, at a banked curve. Our headlights illuminated a round vague space before us in the immense dark space about us, and in that round vague space appeared, suddenly, the bright lights of an oncoming car. It was in the wrong lane. I had a momentary hallucination: that we were not on a highway at all, but had somehow got off, and, wherever it was we were, the space was not defined in any way. We went silent. I saw Germaine's hands tense about the steering wheel; she didn't brake, but, on ice, guided her car round the oncoming car, as if in outer space. Once past the car, she said, "He must have skidded right round on the ice." She had got us through by careful driving. She laughed.

"Open another bottle of champagne," she said.

From time to time she rolled down her window on to the freezing night air because, she said, she was making smelly liquorice farts.

We turned off the highway at a sign for Amarillo on to more broad highways, deserted; there were no buildings on the flat, snow-covered land, illuminated by the lights along the highways. Then, in the far distance, was a group of square buildings lit up green, and about the buildings vast empty parking lots, also lit green. Billowing about the buildings and lots were great clouds of steam.

"What's that?" Germaine asked.

She had asked that about many strange sights; she wanted to know what everything was.

"God knows," I said.

We came to a railway alongside the highway, and a railway yard with open flat cars; the tracks went up to the green-lit buildings.

"I don't understand what it could be," she said.

We saw a sign in green light: BEEF PACKING.

"I should have known," Germaine said.

She drove on, over the icy, empty Amarillo Boulevard, along

which were motels with signs shining high above them; some of
the signs were not working, and the motels appeared to be falling apart.

Germaine said, "We're not going to stay in a motel with a sign
that doesn't work properly."

Slowly, we drove down and then up the wide Boulevard.
Amarillo seemed to have no centre, but to spread out over the
flat, empty land. We stopped at a large motel which looked like a
Swiss chalet.

It was about midnight. Germaine went directly to her room, I
to mine. The motel was silent as if empty. I had a hot shower,
then got into bed. I lay awake for a while, feeling that I was in a
foreign country.

I was glad I was with Germaine.

She woke me at 6.30 by phone from her room. I got up, a bit
lost in the large darkness, and, naked, went to the curtains closed
across a window as wide as the wall; I pulled the cord to the
curtains, which, in little jerks, opened on to an expansive view, in
dawn light, of the motel pool, the ground, shrubs, furniture
about the pool covered in snow, and, beyond low banks of snow,
the highway, where cars with lit parking lights were creeping. I
saw no people, only cars, moving.

I met Germaine in the dining room. We were the only people
there. She was spirited as we looked at maps and marked out the
route. When the waitress came with our eggs, over easy, and
bacon, Germaine had a long talk with her about the conditions of
the roads in New Mexico.

Sometimes, Germaine would be friendly with waiters and
waitresses, and have intimate conversations with them; and
sometimes she would be curt with them, and I saw they served
her grudgingly. I didn't understand why she would be one way
one time, and at another time another way. She seemed to be
unaware of the difference.

This morning she asked the waitress about her work. The
questions might have been those of a researcher trying to compile
statistics on waitresses; and yet I saw the waitress respond as to
someone who took an interest in a job which she herself considered just a dumb way to make money.

When we crossed over into New Mexico, Germaine shouted

out, "Yip, yip, yip, yayee," and leaned forward as she gave the car more gas.

In the bright mid-morning we drank the remaining bottle of champagne.

We were to turn off the highway at Clines Corners; signs appeared, each larger than the one before, announcing Clines Corners where, the signs told us, we should stop to buy Cactus Candy and Cactus Jelly. Clines Corners consisted of one large, windowless, prefabricated building and a gasoline station. We didn't stop for Cactus Candy and Jelly.

Over a narrow road, we drove up into the mountains towards Santa Fé. The country was covered with snow, the surface brilliantly crystallized, and through the snow were visible great swaths of gold plains grass. Beyond the shining white and gold mountains the sky was clear blue.

We went silent driving through the mountains.

Then, rising over a mountain to a view of a valley, Germaine said, "Look at that."

I was enthusiastic for what we saw; and I knew that I could express my enthusiasm because she did hers.

"And look at that," I said.

It was as though—how can I understand this without having recourse to "as though"?—Germaine were educating me to views I had never seen before, and I was, and wanted her to know I was, an enthusiastic pupil.

Looking in all directions not to miss anything, we drove into the small, compact, brown adobe town of Santa Fé.

Our hotel rooms were adjoining, with a locked door between. The high headboards of the beds were painted red with green and yellow Mexican flowers, and at the foot of each bed was a wooden chest painted like the bedsteads.

Germaine said, "Your room is better than mine."

"They look the same to me."

We were in my room. She tried the door between our rooms and said, "We should have this opened."

I became vividly aware of myself standing next to her.

"That's a terrific idea," I said.

On our way to lunch, I stopped at reception and asked the

receptionist please to have the door between Dr Greer's and my
room opened.

She said, "We can't. We've lost the keys, I'm sure. And the
doors between the rooms are painted shut."

I made a face of disappointment at Germaine.

In a Mexican restaurant we had, each of us for the first time,
blue tortillas with our chili. Germaine said they were tasteless,
and the chili was hot without having any flavour.

Then we went out to look. She had to see everything. We went
in and out of every shop along the street the hotel was on, and
around the Plaza. Indians were sitting on the edges of blankets
spread out under the arcade on one side of the Plaza, and on the
blankets were black pots, silver and turquoise jewellery, and
large round loaves in transparent plastic bags. Though Germaine
said, "What a lot of tat," she examined the tat closely. When she
saw an object she thought special, she pointed it out to me.

In a shop, she bought a little turquoise and silver fly, a pin,
which she said was too beautiful not to have. She pinned it to the
lapel of my jacket to stand back and examine it, and as she did she
clasped her hands under her chin and squealed. "It is beautiful,"
she said, then, "Do you want it?" "No, no," I said.

In another shop, she examined closely a San Ildefonso black
bowl held aloft by an elderly woman with blue hair. She said,
"All right, I'll have it." Again, she squealed and clapped her
hands when the bowl, packed in a cardboard box, was handed to
us; I took it to carry. "Do you want to keep it?" she asked. I knew
that if I had said, Yes, thank you, it would have been freely mine.
"No," I said, "thanks."

She said, "I have it, have money, because I'm famous, and I can
earn a lot simply by being famous. Don't worry about it. I'll pay
the big bills. And if you see something you can't afford, tell me,
and I'll buy it for you."

She bought a small hand-made cedar box. She bought a rough
black bowl from an Indian woman under the arcade. She bought
a weathervane for her house in Italy.

Everything we looked at appeared edged with the clear sharp
winter light of New Mexico.

In the shops, people smiled at us. I smiled back. Germaine said,
"You smile, and I find I smile, too. You're going to get me into

the awful American habit of smiling at people when they look at you. You're going to make me as nice as you are."

"I'm not nice," I said.

"So you've told me."

I asked, "And what are you going to do to me?"

Along the narrow street, shop after shop was filled with antiques and paintings and rugs and weaving and pots and specially designed clothes. In the whole of Santa Fé, there seemed to be only one drugstore, one grocery, one Woolworth's; all the other shops were galleries.

Germaine said, "This is Poofterville."

I carried all the packages back to the hotel, and in my room I lay on my bed and fell asleep. From time to time I woke and saw, out of the window, different stages of sunset over the snow-covered adobe town; then I woke to a view of the town outlined along flat roof edges and windowsills with lights flickering in brown paper bags and the night sky dark blue.

At seven I knocked on Germaine's door. She had been typing one of a series of articles she was writing on gardens, under the name of Rose Blight. Gardening books were open on the bed and floor, and papers were everywhere around the little table by the window where she had put her typewriter. She was wearing the red and black check flannel shirt and blue bib overalls she'd been wearing, and she said, "I'll have to wear what I've got on to go to dinner. I forgot my pantihose, so I can't wear my dress." I didn't say, "But I thought you didn't wear underclothes." Perhaps it was too cold. I said, "You give the flannel shirt and jeans real style." She laughed. "Cut the shit," she said; "I look like a fucking mess." At the long mirror on her bathroom door, she took various poses, examining herself. She sighed. "Anyway, let's go eat."

We walked to the restaurant. The night cold was sharp, bright, dry. I kept breathing it in deeply; it burned throughout my sinuses and lungs. Hunched over, Germaine said her ears were freezing. I offered to give her my scarf to tie round her head. "No," she said. I thought that Germaine, when she said no, would mean no. But I offered again, and she said all right. From time to time I grabbed her and rubbed my hands, hard, all over her.

The air smelled of the smoke of piñon fires.

At a corner table in the restaurant, Germaine said, "I'm going to pay for this meal."

The fancy restaurant had a *sommelier* who came with the wine list, which he held out to me. I said, pointing to Germaine, "She'll choose," and he stepped back to look at me and look at Germaine, and, frowning a little, said, "Very well." Germaine ordered a bottle of French wine. After the *sommelier* came back with it and opened it, he began to pour wine into my glass for me to taste it, and I said, "No, she'll try it first," and again he frowned as he poured a little of the wine into Germaine's glass. She said, "It isn't *premier cru*, as it's supposed to be." "It is," he said. "No," she said, "it isn't." He said nothing, staring at her. "However," she said, "it will do, thank you." He poured out a glass for me, then for Germaine.

She said to me, "I know when you're annoyed."

"Do you? What do I do when I'm annoyed?"

"You say, 'No, no, I'm perfectly happy to do anything you want,' and I can tell by the tone of your voice that what you really want to say is, 'Let's stop fucking around, I'm bored going through these fucking shops.'"

I laughed.

"I could tell," she said, "that in the car you felt you couldn't go silent, couldn't withdraw into yourself, but had to keep up a conversation with me, which was a strain on you, and you wished you didn't have to do it."

"Yes," I said. "But I believe in politeness."

"What does that mean?"

"Oh, I take it to mean that the person you're with is more important than you are, and you must go out to him and treat him with the deference he deserves."

"Even if you don't want to? Even if it means being nice when you're not nice?"

"Yep," I said.

She stuck out her lower lip.

With our food, though I can't imagine it was the food which started her off, she talked about her marriage. She described the ceremony and the dinner afterward in a restaurant. She left the party, went to the ladies' room, looked at herself in a mirror and realized she had made a great mistake.

Living with her husband, when she came in from a day out, he would ask, "Where've you been?" and she wouldn't tell him simply because she didn't want to be asked where she'd been or what she'd been doing; she didn't want to feel she had to account to him, and she didn't want to feel guilty for not accounting to him. She hadn't felt, she'd made quite sure she wouldn't feel, guilty towards others since she'd left her mother in Australia.

Then, for most of the meal, she told me about her mother.

I asked her questions. I don't know if I asked her a question she thought offensive—I don't recall if I did—but I recall her all at once looking at me, her face hard, her jaw long, her eyes narrow. Perhaps I had said something which she disapproved of. I certainly felt she disapproved of me, suddenly, entirely. I didn't know what had happened.

We ate in silence for a while. The waiter kept filling our glasses.

Later, with dessert, she told me that she had argued terribly with all her friends, especially her women friends. She raised her head up, so her long neck curved, and she sighed as with relief. She said it always happened that her friends decided, at some point of intimacy, to tell her just what they thought of her: that she was self-involved, and if she considered other people at all it was only as an audience to whom she gave lectures.

She put her fingers over her lips. "They think I can't be hurt. I suppose they imagine I don't know the way I am, and they feel impelled, for some reason which they call friendship but which is their convoluted idea of friendship, to tell me. They don't at all know the way I am."

I wondered if I had said something about her which had hurt her for being so misunderstanding of her.

I said, "But you *do* give the impression that you don't hear, or ever see, the person you're talking to. Whatever I say, for example, seems to produce no reaction in you; and the more important what I have to say is to me, the less you react. Your face becomes stark."

"Does it?"

"I'll tell you, though, that hours, days, sometimes weeks after I might have said something I thought brilliant enough to impress you, and which I imagined didn't, it happens that you'll publicly comment on what I said, and I'll suddenly see you'd been listening closely." I said, "Do you remember the time I made the Anatolian dish with aubergines in Italy? I thought you hadn't taken it in, really, but years later you mentioned that I had taught you to make it, and that you made it often."

She smiled a little with the corners of her mouth.

I still felt I had said something wrong, and I didn't know what it was.

Maybe it had to do with her mother.

We went back to the hotel. In my bed, I couldn't sleep, and I lay wondering why. I knew I felt guilt towards, not all women, but difficult women, and I felt guilt because, somewhere in my life which I could not recall, I had done something, perhaps simply said something, which was wrong, which had hurt them, and the only reaction possible for them to what I had done or said was to be difficult. I had made them difficult.

Yet they gave me something, these women, or at least promised me something, for which I wanted to be close to them. They could justify me in my body and soul.

Germaine rang me in the morning, her voice bright. I ordered breakfast for us both, which we ate, she in her nightgown, by the sunny window in my room.

While she worked on her gardening articles, I went out for a walk. It was Thanksgiving Day. People were gathered about the cathedral; I entered and stood at the back and listened, beyond the congregation, to singers and guitarists at the front of the church singing and playing Mexican songs, and suddenly the double doors by me opened and a procession of Indian women wearing soft leather shoes and embroidered shawls came in, followed by altar boys, then a bishop with a crook. I left, and walked up into the foothills above Santa Fé. The snow on the ground and piñon trees had crystallized, and the dry crystals blew up in small cold bursts of wind, and flashed in the clear sunlight. I walked off the road, into a piñon woods where there were no footmarks but my own. Then I returned to the road, where a one-eyed old Indian in a battered pickup truck stopped to give me a lift, but I told him I was taking a walk, and wished him a happy Thanksgiving.

When I got back to the hotel room I found the door to Germaine's room wide open, and I looked in. She was still in her long nightgown, barefoot, watching a maintenance man try different large keys on a ring in the lock of the door between our rooms. One opened the door and Germaine jumped up, clapped her hands, and squealed.

She said to me, "I got him to do it."

The maintenance man smiled.

A thrill of fear passed through me.

We left the door open.

It was as if I were naked, and, self-consciously naked, I sat on her bed while she sat in an armchair, and I told her about my morning.

She got up from her chair. "I guess I'd better get ready to go out," she said. "I'll have to wear what I wore yesterday."

A student of ours had, from Tulsa, rung up a friend of hers in Santa Fé, an elderly woman, who through our student had invited Germaine and me to Thanksgiving lunch. At first Germaine said, "I've spoken to too many people, and I don't want to speak to anyone now. You can do it. You can be among people who even bore you and put on an act that they're the most interesting people you've ever met. I can't." She shrugged. "Well, let's go. No doubt we'll have turkey. I hate turkey, a tasteless bird which has all the tasteless qualities of this country." I said, "We'll only do what you want to do. Honestly. I'd rather. I want to do what's most restful for you, and if, after your weeks of lecture tours and thousands of people to talk to, you'd prefer to have a sandwich here in our rooms, I'd like that." "No," she said, "we'll go."

On a map of Santa Fé I found the street where we were to go. It did not appear far, and I suggested to Germaine that we walk. Outside the hotel she asked, "Which way?" It occurred to me that every time we left the hotel Germaine asked, "Which way?" and did not know her way back to the hotel. I was surprised that she should be so disorientated (to stick to my guns), and I was surprised, too, that she was amused and not annoyed when I, turning the map in all directions, got lost. I stopped a big car to ask directions; the driver, a young Indian, took us to the street. Germaine kept laughing.

Our hostess was short, plump, in a long black dress, her white hair tied up at the side of her head in Hopi fashion. She introduced us to other guests, two women, one with a little boy, and a male high-school teacher. From the living-room window of the cottage was a wide view of a snow-covered mountain crossed by thirty-six (Germaine counted them out loud) electricity cables.

We sat. Our hostess gave us wine. We were silent.

Germaine said, "Do I smell turkey? How wonderful! We're having turkey!"

I smiled.

When our hostess and the high-school teacher and the little boy went into the kitchen, I followed them to help.

From the living room I heard Germaine talking to the other women as if giving a lecture.

At table, the hostess asked Germaine, "What is it like to be a cult figure?"

"I'll tell you what it means," she said. "It means that people who don't know your work at all, so have no idea what you stand for, presume that they do, and insist on discussing your work with you. What I really want, and don't have, is the respect of my peers. For whatever reason, and it could be jealousy, my peers are suspicious of me, and don't respect me."

We sat in the living room afterwards, Germaine and I together on the sofa. The sun set. Two middle-aged men with moustaches came in; they were interior decorators and lived together. Germaine and I often touched one another as they watched us. While we talked, she held one of my hands in hers and with her other rubbed my arm for a long time as with a great warm affection and familiarity.

One of the men asked me if I knew a certain young British painter.

I thought a moment. "Yes," I said, "I do."

"He comes to Santa Fé often," the other man said.

"I knew that," I said.

"He had an exhibition here last year," the first said, "with a drawing of you in it."

"Really?"

I was very attentive to Germaine. After three hours there I saw she was tired. I put an arm round her and said we should go. She nodded and sighed.

She sighed a great deal.

The high-school teacher gave us a lift back to the hotel.

That evening in my room we watched television, one stupid programme after another. In her nightgown, Germaine sat in an armchair and knitted; I lay on my bed, my feet at the top, my head at the bottom, pillows under my elbows. Germaine kept getting up to change the channels, saying, "What shit American television is." She came to the musical *The Sound of Music*, and we watched a bit of it, both saying, "This is awful, awful, awful," and Germaine changed to other channels, but more awful programmes appeared, and we always came round to *The Sound of Music*, which, after all, we watched. The governess to a family of unhappy Austrian children wants to make them happy, and she does this by contriving clothes for all of them out of the flowered curtains of her bedroom; happy in their new clothes, they go out into the whole of Switzerland, singing. I saw Germaine lower her knitting to her lap as she watched the governess lead the children up into the green mountains, all of them singing to the sky. Then she turned to me, her lower lip stuck out; tears were dripping down her face, and she wiped them away with the back of her hand. She said, "This is shit," and got up and changed the channel.

We slept with the door open between our rooms.

In the morning, out of the bath and wrapped in a towel, I passed the open door and saw Germaine, dressing. She grabbed the fat round her waist and squeezed it into a roll. "Look at that," she said. Then she slapped her behind. "I've gone slack-assed." She pulled up the skin on her thigh and said, "That's gone crêpey."

While she worked on her gardening articles, I went out to bookshops. I looked for and found her books in the shops.

After lunch in a Mexican restaurant, where Germaine said only the guacamole was good, we drove off in the car to tour the country round Santa Fé.

We stopped at the Pueblo San Ildefonso, a low ring of adobe houses about a vast sandy plaza in which, off-centre, was a round stone platform. Nailed to a tree at the entrance to the pueblo was a sign: KEEP OFF THE KIVA. "What's a kiva?" Germaine asked. "I don't know," I said. The pueblo appeared deserted. We went into a part adobe, part corrugated-iron shed, a gift shop, where an

Indian, behind a counter with a few ugly bowls, simply looked at us. In a whisper, I said to Germaine, 'I'll ask him what a kiva is." She frowned. "No," she said. "I'd better," I said, "or we won't know what to keep off." There was a flash of anger in her eyes, and I wondered why. I asked the man, who said in a low, slack voice that the kiva was the stone platform in the plaza, and that it was used for ceremonies. Germaine pointed to the bowls and said they were lovely, when I knew she knew they were ugly. I realized she said it because she was embarrassed, and when we got out of the shop it came to me that she was perhaps embarrassed because she hadn't wanted the man to know she was ignorant of what a kiva was, and she'd been angry at me for a moment because, by asking, I revealed to the man that she was ignorant. We walked across the empty plaza, over which sand blew up, past the kiva and to a large, twisted, bare tree which Germaine said must be the Council Oak. In front of some of the houses, which had porches with carved pillars and cross-beams, were beehive ovens, and as we went by them I felt heat come off them. But we still saw no one. Dogs barked.

We were to meet the elderly woman who'd given us Thanksgiving lunch, and two of her friends, at a restaurant in Chimayo for dinner, but we got lost. At a gasoline station, I asked directions to Chimayo, and, again, I saw Germaine get angry.

Early after all, we sat in the bar of the restaurant and ordered tequila. Germaine said, referring to the woman we were to meet, "I hope her two friends are poofs. I wouldn't be able to take two heavy ladies." We ordered more tequila. We were sitting by a fireplace in which piñon logs were burning. A moment of intimacy seemed to encircle us. From time to time I'd reach out and touch her, or lean towards her and kiss her.

The elderly woman came with an academic husband and wife.

In Santa Fé, before we went to our rooms, we walked around the Plaza, under the arcades, to fart out, Germaine said, the gas from the beans of all the bad Mexican food we'd eaten. She stopped, or I stopped, to fart, then, laughing, we continued.

I was drunk, and threw off my clothes and got into bed.

Saturday morning, our last full day, we went out to look through the shops we hadn't been into.

The first shop was filled with fur coats. As Germaine was looking at them, an old thin man wearing a toupee approached as if to take from Germaine's hands the coat she was examining. She still wore her check flannel shirt and bib overalls and jogging shoes. She asked the man, "How much is this?" He said something like, "Forty-three thousand dollars." "I want to try it on," she said. He helped her on with it, and Germaine strode about the shop, swinging the coat, and pausing at mirrors to look at it on her. I said, "That's beautiful, Germaine," and I found myself emphasizing her name so the man in the toupee might twig who was in his shop. She said, "I'm not sure." She tried on other furs, all expensive, which the man helped her with. Again and again, I'd say, "Germaine—," because I wanted the old man to know I was with someone on whom, if he knew, he would have waited with deferential attention. She said to the man, "I don't think any will do, really." "Very well," he said. We left.

In the sunlight, the snow was melting and dripping from the adobe roofs.

I asked, "Would you really have bought a fur coat if you'd found one you liked?"

"I was just playing," she said. She sprinted a little ahead of me, along a street. When I got to her she clapped her hands and said, "We're going to do a lot of playing in the shops."

We went into shop after shop up and down Canyon Road, and Germaine, it seemed to me, looked at every single item, even every bad painting. Often she'd point out a bit of weaving or pottery, Indian and old, and say, "Look." About turquoise, she said she was pretty tired of it (and she had by now learned the names of all the different kinds and where each was from), but when, in one shop, she saw in a glass case a bracelet of silver and mellow greenish turquoise, she said to me, "Look at that. It's very moving."

I laughed.

She said, "You see, I *am* becoming like you."

In another shop she tried on Ecuadorean ponchos. The saleslady, who wore many silver and turquoise bracelets, recognized Germaine, and said, "We're very impressed." A lot of attention was given to her also by other salespeople in the shop. Germaine often hugged me and kissed me. With each poncho, she asked me, "What do you think of this one?" The sales people looked at me, and I could see in their eyes the wonder: Is this Germaine Greer's lover? She bought the poncho I specially liked, one woven in delicate stripes of white, pale blue and pale pink. She went out wearing it.

We were on Canyon Road till, at sunset, the dripping snow began to freeze into icicles.

She bought yards of Guatemalan fabric and a Rio Grande rug.

I had to pee, and went behind an adobe house and peed into a bank of snow.

Germaine called, "Can I watch?"

As I was coming out of my bathroom to go to bed, I passed the open door and saw Germaine in bed, the blankets pulled up to her chin. I stopped at the doorway.

In a moment of intense self-consciousness, so great I was not sure who I was, I said, "Good night."

"Good night," she said.

I got into bed.

Whenever I woke, I heard her breathing in the next room.

Germaine insisted on paying the hotel bill. "It doesn't matter," she said. "I have the money."

We left in the bright cold morning while Santa Fé was sleeping to drive up through the mountains to Taos. The red-pink earth showed where the snow was melting.

She asked me, "Do you think you would ever kill yourself?"

"No. Never."

"Did you ever try?"

"I've often thought about it, but, no, I've never tried."

"I once did," she said, "when I was a teenager. I was wearing my father's greatcoat, which I loved, and which was much too big for me, so I had to clutch it about my body. I was very depressed. I was depressed, deeply, deeply depressed, because I had thought out that there was no God. I thought, though, that I'd give God a chance to prove Himself, and, in my father's greatcoat, I walked along the edge of a cliff, allowing myself to teeter, and I thought, if there were a God, He would save me, and if there weren't I'd fall over and die, which was what I wanted, anyway, if there were no God. I fell. I fell and rolled down a steep bank, and I tried to keep myself from rolling further by clutching at branches. Finally, I stopped rolling, a long way down. And I was very upset because I had torn my father's greatcoat."

I tried to see her at that age. I tried to see her at any age younger than the age of her public image, and I couldn't. That the present large Germaine might contain a past small Germaine who wanted to die did not seem possible to me. Whatever had happened to change her from a small girl into a large women, the change had been essential; she did not think inwardly about herself, but outwardly about the world.

We passed through the high strange mountain towns of Truchas and Trampas. In all directions, the mountains rose and rose.

I risked asking her, "Don't you want a long lasting relationship with someone?"

"There's nothing I'd like more," she said, "but I get bored by people after a very short time."

"Are you getting bored with me?"

"Yes, I am."

I laughed.

"So you'll never commit yourself to a relationship?"

She glanced to the side at me, but said nothing.

At dusk, we stopped in the Oklahoma panhandle for gasoline. A little blond boy came out of the station to put the nozzle of the hose into the car tank; the pump looked broken down, and the numbers rolled quickly, and soon the price was up to twenty-five dollars. I said to Germaine, "The last time we got gas, we filled it up, and I paid, and I know I didn't pay more than fifteen dollars." Her eyes snapped open on me. "Don't make a federal case out of it," she said. I stepped back. The price went up to thirty-five dollars. The little boy kept his hand on the nozzle; I heard not gasoline but air pumped out. I dared myself to say, "There's something wrong." Germaine said sharply to me, "Cut it out, will you? Just cut it out." I turned and walked away and wandered about the old gasoline station. I saw her go into the illuminated station and, through a wide window, I saw her talk to a man in greasy overalls. When she came out she laughed a little and said, "You were right."

I was silent in the car.

At Woodward, just off the Oklahoma panhandle, we stopped again for gasoline, and from there Germaine, taking swigs from a bottle of Jack Daniel, drove on to Tulsa, normally a six-hour drive, in three hours. I did not look at the speedometer. I was frightened, and held myself still.

A week or so after we got back, Germaine gave a lecture at the Unitarian Church in Tulsa on abortion and contraception. The long church hall was filled. In front of me was a mother with her two teenage girls. Powerful lights illuminated the stage so TV cameras could film the lecture; in the intense light, Germaine appeared to have a burning silver sheen about her. As she talked, she moved her arms in loose, soft gestures, and I found myself being drawn in, not to a public argument in support of abortion as she defined it, but a private revelation about love. It was as if, moving her arms, Germaine had begun to sing, and the aria, about deeply private passions and regrets, happiness and pain, rose up and up and out. I thought: She's talking about herself. And yet she wasn't talking about herself. She was talking about the outside world, and in her large awareness of it, she knew it as I did not; it was as if she had a secret knowledge of it, and to learn that secret from her would make me a different person. I wanted to be a different person. I had never heard Germaine give a public lecture; I had never seen her so personal. I thought: I love her.

At our Thursday luncheon in the Greek restaurant Germaine said to me, "You like difficult women, don't you?"

I said in a Tulsan accent, "I guess I do."

"Well then," she said, "I'll introduce you to my mother."

The Three

JEAN RHYS, born Ella Gwendolen Rees Williams,
1890 or 1894.
(She has never revealed her age. The record office in
Roseau, Dominica, where she was born, burned down
and with it her birth certificate.)

SONIA ORWELL, born 1918.
GERMAINE GREER, born 1939.

A

abortion

In Jean's day it was called "an illegal operation". She writes in her autobiography that, after the operation, "I didn't suffer from remorse or guilt. I didn't think at all like women are supposed to think, my predominant feeling was one of intense relief, but I was very tired. I was not at all unhappy. It was like a pause in my life, a peaceful time."

She resists identifying herself, even in having an abortion, with other women. The abortion is entirely personal, and she does not give it much thought.

Sonia, I believe, sees abortion as an of course.

Germaine sees abortion as a political as well as a personal issue. She has thought out the issue very carefully and articulates her thoughts carefully.

In her office at the back of the Center, I see, spread out on her desk, multicoloured propaganda put about by the anti-abortionists; I pick up a pamphlet on which are photographs of a pile of aborted babies in a black plastic garbage can and of an adult's hand holding the two tiny feet, perfectly formed, of an aborted foetus. I say, "How upsetting these pictures are," and expect Germaine to tell me I don't understand, but she says, "It is very deeply upsetting. They are entirely right to make us aware of the horror of abortion, because it is horrible."

Germaine considers the effects of abortion on, not simply women, but women in the United States, women in Italy, women in India.

alcohol

Germaine will clutch the fat at her tummy and shake it and say, "That's alcohol."

Sonia never drinks spirits, only wine. She does not mind plonk. If, when she comes to dinner, she sees, for four people, five uncorked bottles, she may ask, "Is that all the wine there is?" and if you say yes, she may say, "Look, could you go out to buy two more bottles just to be sure?" and try to press the money on you. In the future, you make sure you have three bottles of wine for Sonia.

She says, "I'm not an alcoholic. I'm a drunkard. An alcoholic drinks with a hangover. A drunkard can't bear to."

As for Jean, she imagines she survives on drink.

animals

When Germaine visits Jean in her cottage in Devon, she suggests Jean should have a cat or a kitten. Jean says she'll have to think about it; she doesn't quite know how to feed a cat, or a delicate kitten. Sonia says, "Jean have a pet? It would die the way her son died, because she wouldn't know how to take care of it."

She feeds birds crumbs one hard winter, then she sees that cats wait, crouched in the bushes until she goes into the house, to pounce on the feeding birds; she gives up feeding the birds.

She likes to look out of her window at cows in a distant field.

Animals seem not to come into Sonia's life at all. She does not like cats to be near her, and asks you when she visits please to put the cats in another room.

In London, Germaine takes the cat of friends who no longer want him. He is ill, and she keeps him alive for two years with special care. When, finally, she has to take him to the vet to be put down, she insists on holding him in her lap. As she tells the story, her eyes fill with tears and she wipes them away with her knuckles.

B

babies
Jean's son dies as an infant, the daughter grows to maturity raised by her father in another country. Jean cannot take care of babies.

I cannot imagine Sonia having a baby; it is as if it were a physical impossibility.

Germaine has made public requests for a man to give her a baby. She tells me this story: Peeking into a bedroom, she saw her then lover whacking off, and said, "What the fuck are you doing?", to which he replied, "I'm getting good and ready to give you the baby you want," and she laughed.

A sense emanates from her of being able to have many babies whom she would hold to her, all together, all the time: babies in her arms, under her arms, between her breasts, playing about her thighs.

blacks
Jean's relationship to blacks is, I think, more complex than her relationship with her family.

In the toilet in a train in France, Sonia sees, scribbled on the wall, "*Les nègres ont les lèvres épais et le nez plat.*" She tries to rub it off with a wet tissue, but can't. As she leaves, a black man is waiting outside to go in, and she is worried what his reaction to the graffito will be.

Walking across the Tulsa University campus, Germaine says, "Look at that beautiful black, walking in an electric-blue aura of sex. Look at him. That's what I want. You bet. I want big black nigger cock."

bodies
Jean, I think, rather likes her body and is not modest. I see her often wearing a nightgown under which she is naked and, as she lurches from chair back to chair back across the room, her small twisted body may appear through the nightgown against a lamp.

Yet, she will dictate passages about having to bathe her body, spray it with talc, dress it, and get it on to the street where she feels she is pushing it along like a wheelbarrow.

As I arrive and when I leave her, she raises her thin arms high and wide, ready to hug me as I advance towards her to embrace her.

Sonia does not like to be touched. When one embraces her, she presents her cheek near her ear and winces a little. She appears to be very clean.

Germaine seems to be very much at ease in her large body. Her fingernails are usually dirty.

business sense

Jean has none.

In discussing certain litigation with her, Sonia's lawyer asks if she hasn't some friends in business who might have advised her in her dealings with the George Orwell Estate. She, angry, replies, "Of course I don't have business friends! Of course not!"

On 17 May 1980, this item appears in the *Sunday Telegraph*:

SONIA ORWELL'S CASH MYSTERY

Friends of Mrs Sonia Orwell, widow of the novelist George Orwell, were trying last night to discover where most of her fortune of nearly £290,000 went.

Mrs Orwell, who married the writer shortly before his death in 1950, died aged 63 last December leaving estate in this country valued at £289,109 gross, but only £37,800 net. She lived in Paris.

A close friend of hers said last night it was not clear why the net estate was so small. "I think there may have been a tax problem, and that is probably where most of the money from the estate has gone."

In Tulsa, Germaine talks of investing money in oil, but she doesn't do it. If she has a business sense, she doesn't act on it.

C

children

Sonia has a godson whom she talks about with great excitement.

"I took him to Hampstead Heath. He wanted to run a race. I told him I'd beat him, but he told me he'd beat me. We started off, over the heath. I had to put everything into it, and nearly collapsed in the end, but I beat him."

Germaine complains often that the children of friends are not being properly looked after. When she has parents and their children as guests, she takes over the children, feeds them what she believes the right food for them, insists they go to bed at the right times, are engagingly entertained, and are disciplined.

Jean can have brief, lively conversations with children, treating them as equals; she doesn't quite know how to treat children as children—unlike Sonia, who, with children, herself becomes a little childlike.

class

With Jean, the change from middle class to whatever class she now is is not intentional, but where her life has brought her.

(She has a great belief that her life has been all along out of her hands and in the hands of Fate.)

I imagine that Sonia does not so much turn against her middle class as be drawn into the class of writers and painters she meets in London.

Germaine has made statements in the revolutionary magazines of the Sixties, *Oz* and *Suck*, advocating the destruction of the middle class, from which she comes.

clothes

Jean dresses up and puts on makeup to write. She has one long purple-pink dress that clings to her, with sleeves which, when she lifts her arms, spread open into wings. After she has worn a dress a very few times, she never wears it again. She says, "*They* don't understand. Yes, I have pretty dresses. But a new dress boosts my morale. I need to have new pretty dresses." She comes up to London to buy dresses, though it exhausts her to be taken to the shops. The purple-pink dress is replaced by one with a bold flower pattern; it has a full skirt, a wide floppy collar and puffed sleeves. She has a number of wigs, one blond-pink, which she sends out to be "done". In a pretty dress and wig, she stands, one hand on a chair back, the other on a hip, and you are quite sure she is, for a moment, posing, waiting for you to say something.

Though Sonia says she absolutely understands Jean's need for clothes, she herself has little need for them. She dresses plainly, usually in a blouse with a lace collar and long sleeves and a skirt. You are more aware of her clothes, plain, and not expensive, than the body they cover. Sonia's clothes don't suggest her body. Sometimes her clothes are worn and darned in patches. She has one winter overcoat.

Germaine knows all about designer clothes, and recognizes on other women designers' styles. Hung in the back seat of the car on the way to Santa Fé is a dress which sways with the movements of the car; she tells me who designed it, but I forget. In her room I see it thrown on the floor by her bed. In what is considered the best clothes shop in Tulsa, she finds a designer sweater, but, she says, the shoulder pads have been taken out, and while she waits the shoulder pads are found and sewn back in so she can buy the sweater and walk out wearing it. She wears a sweatsuit to a dinner party.

cooking

An actress visiting Jean for the first time, in London, is amazed that there is no food in the house. When Max comes in he does not appear surprised that there is nothing to eat, or drink. The actress goes out for drink. They all go later to a restaurant.

Jean's characters, in boarding houses, are often brought cheese and bread or boiled onions to their rooms.

In Devon, Jean has someone cook for her. When an unexpected visitor arrives she reluctantly offers tea and hopes the offer won't be accepted as she'll have to make the tea, a tedious job, and do the washing up, a more tedious job.

She eats very little, but likes spicy food.

Sonia is knowledgeable about and gives a lot of attention to her cooking, which is mostly French. Though she drinks plonk at friends' houses, her own wine is very good. Her table is always set with bright silver, lovely china, shining crystal, and starched white linen, with flowers in the centre. She eats very little of her own cooking, and criticizes it. She smokes between courses.

In Italian provincial restaurants, she wants to try dishes she has never had before.

Germaine writes articles about cookery. The kitchen in her flat in London is scientifically organized for cooking properly.

country
Jean was born and brought up in Dominica, an island in the West Indies. Sonia in India. Germaine in Australia. None seem to have any real country to which they belong.

Jean talks with nostalgia about France, but she doesn't want to go there because she is frightened it might have all changed. She will not go back to Dominica because she is sure that has changed. "There are no longer any roses there! Not even roses left!"

Sonia, in London, has many French friends who stay with her when they come over, and who are, I imagine, kept apart by Sonia as belonging to a somewhat superior society. "My French friends," she says. She often interjects French into her talk. When, as if going to the one country where she might belong, she goes to Paris, she writes to her friends in London please to come visit her as she is lonely.

Germaine travels a great deal in many countries, except Australia, where she goes rarely.

D

depression
Like her characters, Jean is largely depressed. She has, often, terrible "*cafards*", and she does not keep them to herself. Sometimes you suspect the depression is an affectation. She does not seem to question her depression, or blame it on herself; she blames the world.

Deeply depressed as she is, Sonia keeps her depression to herself. I imagine she gets out of bed, washes, puts on makeup, goes out to shop, all in the darkness of her depression, to create a bright dinner party for her friends. During the dinner, she gets angry at one of her friends—"What a stupid thing to say"—and ruins the party.

Germaine, I notice, sighs a lot.

divorce

Each is divorced: Jean from her first husband, Jean Lenglet, after thirteen years of marriage. She remarries twice; both husbands die. Sonia, the widow of George Orwell, marries Michael Pitt-Rivers, and divorces him after four years. Germaine marries Paul de Feux and divorces him after three weeks.

domesticity

Not until friends go to Jean's cottage in Devon to decorate it is anything done to make it pretty. She is used to drab rooms, and, unable to change them, she concentrates on details with which to enliven them: a picture, a ceramic leopard, a glass paperweight. But these are mostly gifts. Moving from place to place, she loses things.

She is not able to make a home for herself.

In London, Sonia has a large house. The parquet floors are highly polished and reflect the light through the high, clean windows. There are shelves and shelves filled with books, and vases of fresh flowers on tables. After she sells the house, stores her furniture, and moves to Paris, she lives in a small rented room with a large turn-of-the-century armoire; the walls she has had painted pale cream, she has a lace counterpane on the bed, an Indian print cloth over the awkward round table, and vases of flowers.

Germaine designs her living spaces in London and Italy, where she hardly ever is. In Tulsa, she lives at the back of a garden in a little one-room building. The heating doesn't work. She says she doesn't mind, and rather likes her small white room.

The domestic spaces for all three women are not in any way determined by family life.

E

education
In Dominica, Jean is taught by nuns in a convent school. When she is sixteen, she is sent to England and the Perse School for girls in Cambridge. She is not there for long before she leaves to go to the Academy of Dramatic Arts, where, again, she stays for a short time.

Sonia is a boarding student at a convent school; I do not know what other, if any, formal education she has.

Germaine also goes to a convent school. Later, a student of Leavis, she gets her Ph. D. from Cambridge. Her special interest is Renaissance literature.

emotions
Jean expresses her emotions with abandon, and, when drunk, wildly.

In person, Sonia finds it very difficult to express emotions, except for anger. Her letters are filled with expressions of feeling.

Germaine expresses her feelings fully, then, suddenly, not at all.

F

feminism
A Portuguese friend, male, asks me if I will help get signatures for a petition protesting the arrest, in Portugal, of three women writers called the Three Marias, for a book they have written together. I take the petition to a tea party at Sonia's; she signs it, as do other female and male guests. Jean, wearing a hat, is there, and when I ask her if she'd like to sign, she looks out, her eyes large and unfocused. "Will you explain it to me?" she asks. I explain. She is still bewildered, but says, "If you think it's all right." Hesitantly, she signs. Sometime later I see an article in *Time* magazine about the Three Marias having been released from arrest. Sometime after that I hear the Three Marias have quarrelled among themselves, and when I tell this to Jean, she shrugs.

Sonia does not consider feminism in the abstract. She proposes, at a feminist meeting, the establishment of day nurseries for working mothers. Some militant women object that the important issues are not being discussed, and they stop the meeting.

Often, when I am in public places with Germaine, young and elderly women come to her to say, simply, "*The Female Eunuch* meant a great deal to me," or, "Your book changed my life." She answers, "I'm sure you would have thought out the change on your own."

A publisher mentions to Germaine an anthology of women's poetry edited by three women in California. She says she knows it. He says, "They argued violently over it." She says, "You surprise me!" Her voice is flat and bitter. "Women arguing violently among themselves! Is that possible? Women are meant to support one another, not fight one another. I *am* surprised."

friends

Sonia has a large group of friends, keeps in close touch with them, and invites them often to her house to dinner. She likes having long lunches with friends to discuss and advise on, say, changing a publisher, buying a new flat, or problems with close relationships; she not only likes this, she becomes obsessed with these things. She refuses to discuss her own problems; her friends' problems become hers, and she discusses them while smoking a pack of cigarettes and drinking three bottles of wine. She is obsessed, too, with talking about mutual friends, but she has this rule: only the closest mutual friends are discussed, and nothing is repeated. Sonia lives in terms of her friends. She is highly critical of them.

Germaine claims to have no friends, but many people claim to be friends of her. She does not stay in touch with anyone.

I wonder if Germaine has a proper address book.

Jean counts on friends getting in touch with her.

She loves receiving letters, but does not like talking over the telephone. She always answers letters from friends.

She doesn't gossip about her friends, and if you say something a little critical of a mutual friend she frowns as if she cannot imagine how you can be a friend of someone and be critical of him.

Any criticism—or even anger—she might have towards an individual friend comes out as an angry criticism of a generalized "them".

G

generalizations

Jean's generalizations about "people" are vast, and arise out of very private obsessions.

Sonia will say, "The French are. . . ," "The Americans are. . . ," "The English are. . .", as if to sum up whole cultures in a generalization. Her generalizations are made with such enthusiasm, sometimes such vehement enthusiasm, you don't dispute them. They arise out of her knowledge of the world.

In conversation, Germaine makes very few generalizations, and when she does she qualifies them. If I generalize, she says, "Now wait . . ."

gifts

Jean is reassured by gifts, and also likes to give them: a shirt, a scarf, a bottle of cologne. But she is not sure you like what she has given you, as you are not quite sure she likes what you have given her.

Sonia does not enjoy being given a gift. She says thank you, but, you think, quickly pushes it aside, and you're sure she gives it to someone else. She only enjoys giving, and her gifts are expensive: a cashmere pullover, for example, or a suit.

When I give Germaine a little gift, I am struck by how appreciative she is; I'm struck, I realize, because she appears to be someone who does not need gifts. Then I leave a packet of mastic from Chios on her desk, as I know she likes to chew it as gum; for days she doesn't mention it until I ask her, and she says, surprised, "Oh yes," and I think she thinks I am testing her for a conventional response, which she won't give. The next day I find a gift from her on my desk.

God and the Virgin and saints
Jean was drawn to Catholicism when she was young. Sonia, in a convent school, and Germaine, also in a convent school, were brought up as Catholics.

Jean is a vague agnostic.

Sonia is an atheist.

I imagine this about Germaine: that whether or not God exists in His own right she thinks is not very interesting, but what has been made of Him is.

The same for the Virgin.

"I went to Lourdes," Germaine says, "in the middle of the winter, and found in the grotto where the Virgin appeared spring roses in blossom. I made requests to relieve the sufferings of three friends."

Jean, I think, has a belief in saints, if not in God.

H

homosexuality
Drunk, Jean says all people are bisexual. I am sure she is simply repeating what someone, not too long ago, has told her; she does not seem very interested.

Many of Sonia's close male friends are homosexual.

She does not like to be touched by men, homosexual or not, but embraces women easily. She is more at ease with women than men.

In lectures, Germaine mentions "the lessons which can be learned from our homosexual brothers and sisters". Privately, she says, "I think it is a sin."

About long-lasting homosexual relationships, she says, "I should make a study of them to try to find out how they work," as if she might from them extract a principle of social behaviour.

humour
Jean likes funny stories. She tells this story: her husband Max, with a friend, was sent during the First World War to Malta, where they got drunk and were stopped by a policeman; when Max said, "Balls," the policeman said, "One does not say 'Balls'

to the police of Malta." Jean laughs and laughs, and holds both hands to her mouth. She will tell the story over and over, and laugh in the same way each time.

With some effort, Sonia laughs; most often she simply says, "How funny," and smiles. She finds most amusing the oddities of her friends.

Germaine's laugh can be a little wicked when a story is told against someone.

She laughs when she farts.

I

individuals and society
Jean addresses herself to the individual.

Germaine addresses society.

In Sonia, a confusion of the two.

intelligence
Jean has, I imagine, an intuitive intelligence; it is not structured, but flashes.

Sonia has great admiration for intelligence, and is intimidated by people whom she considers her intellectual superiors.

When discussing a topic, Sonia does not so much analyse it as exhaust it.

Germaine's intelligence is structured and trained.

J

Jews
I think that to Jean, Jews are foreign and exotic. Her closest friends in Paris are a Jewish family.

Around the table at a dinner party at Sonia's are, among others, Jewish writers. There is a pause in the conversation, and Sonia, flicking her ash, says to one of her guests, not a Jew, "Is it true your father couldn't stand Jews?" He, who will not excuse his father, says, in a long drawl, "It's absolutely true. He couldn't stand having a Jew in the same room with him." Sonia says, "I thought so." This is to demonstrate such a total lack of prejudice that in her house anything can be said. She believes one should be able to say, "That fucking Jew", in the same way one might say, "That fucking Scot." She is very pro-Israeli.

At a party with Germaine, a large Jewish man asks her, "Are you Jewish?" She answers in what I presume to be Yiddish. He says, "I thought you were."

jobs

Jean's writing is the only work she is capable of. All other minor attempts at work fail.

In the world of literature, Sonia has a job, for a short period, as fiction editor at a publishing house. She is pleased to publish good writing, but she is also aware that she must publish books which sell; she takes on a certain novel not merely because it is a good book but also, she is sure, because it will sell; it does.

She works as one of the editors of a magazine of art and literature, owned by friends.

She translates from the French the work of writers who are her friends.

Germaine works as a writer, teacher, lecturer, reviewer, board member of a women's press, journal editor, and cultivator, in Italy, of iris plants for the orris roots.

justice

For Sonia, there are brave attempts made at social justice, and she would and does help in every attempt she believes in, but, finally, there is no social justice.

She goes to the concentration camp at Dachau with a French friend, who is horrified. Sonia, angry, says, "What did you expect? What? That it wouldn't be quite as horrible as you imagined? Well, this is just the beginning of the horrors."

Sonia organizes letter protests, and is always willing to sign petitions against the imprisonment and torturing of intellectuals; but she does not think this will do much good.

I imagine that Germaine does not believe there is much justice in the world, but lives must be saved.

Jean believes there is a world conspiracy against justice.

L

literature
Jean, the writer, has read little.

When I suggest to Sonia that she should write, she shakes her head no, absolutely no.

Sonia is telling Jean and me about a book she has just read and mentions what she imagines to be the writer's intention. Jean and I say, together, "No, that can't really be the intention of a writer," and Sonia narrows her eyes and says, "*Tiens*, that goes to show how little I know about writing."

There is no author I mention whose work she has not read—or whom, if he or she is alive, she does not know.

In Paris, she is reading masses of Victor Hugo, who is, she writes in a letter, marvellous.

It is as if for Sonia man could do nothing greater than write books.

Germaine's favourite reading, she tells me, is Ariosto's *Orlando Furioso*.

love

_____

loyalty
Jean is loyal to friends.

In some way, Sonia feels responsible for her friends. If they are unhappy, she does what she can to cheer them up; if they are ill, she takes them to her doctor or pays to have them stay in a clinic; if they are in debt, she will go as far as writing to other friends to raise the large sum of money needed to clear the debt.

Germaine is loyal.

M

machines
There is not one machine Jean can use.

Without understanding how they work, Sonia can use them.

Germaine understands them as she uses them.

men
_____

mind
Jean's mind, I believe, is and always has been stubbornly fixed.
She know she is not wrong in what she thinks.
  Sonia does not change her mind easily, but she does.
  Germaine often changes her mind.

money
As little as she has had of it—or because she has had so little—Jean
seems not to relate money to work. One works and gets little,
most likely nothing; money simply occurs suddenly, and is
unrelated to what one has or has not done. It is quickly gone, and
she has no idea where. She worries a lot about not having it.
  Sonia feels she has not earned the money she gets from the
George Orwell Estate, and spends a great deal of it on others.
  Germaine works for her money.

music
I take Jean to Harrods record department to buy some records for
the long dreary winter in Devon. She buys an Ella Fitzgerald
record, Chopin's *Marche funèbre* ("Do you think it might be a little
morbid in Devon?"), and South American rumbas and tangos
("They'll soothe me"). She has no general knowledge of music.
  Sonia does not listen to music unless a friend is singing,
playing, conducting.
  At my flat, Germaine picks up a book of madrigals, and, with
nothing better to do, sings madrigal after madrigal.

N

news
Though she reads the newspapers and watches the reports on
television, the news seems to make no sense to Jean—that is, she
cannot recount the news she has just read or seen and heard—until

one incident inflames her, and the incident becomes the news of all the world.

Sonia and Germaine know what is going on in the world. Though Sonia does not imagine there is anything that can be done for the world, Germaine does.

P

painting

Jean has no knowledge of painting. She may like a painting because it is a cheerful yellow.

Through her painter friends, Sonia has a small, precious collection: Lucien Freud, Francis Bacon—

After dinner one evening a woman writer invited for the first time admires a little painting over Sonia's desk. Sonia says, "That's of me, by William Coldstream." She takes it off the wall and hands it to the writer. "I can't," the writer says. "Yes, yes, you must," Sonia says; "I don't like having pictures of myself around." The writer gently takes the painting in her hands.

I arrive at Sonia's for tea. Other people are there and they, gathered around a table, are examining, on the fly leaf of a large book about Picasso, a pencil drawing in red, yellow, blue by Picasso which is made of the words À SONIA. "We've had enough of that," Sonia says, and slams the book shut.

She repeats what her painter friends say about painters and exhibitions.

Germaine has published a reference book on women painters.

parties

Jean loves going to parties. She sits quietly in the centre and people lean towards her and talk. For periods no one speaks to her, and she stares out.

In London, Sonia gives big parties, sometimes for people she considers of high distinction: Papandreou, Lacan. She does not appear to like these parties.

Though she may say she doesn't want to go, Germaine goes to parties.

She says, "Maybe I'll meet the man of my dreams," and laughs.

At parties, she has a group, mostly women, listening to her.

photographs

There are very few surviving early photographs of Jean. She does not take to being photographed, and wants to see the proofs to choose the one or two she thinks best; she asks that the others be destroyed.

Sonia does not like to keep photographs of anyone, least of all herself.

There is a famous photograph of Germaine in the nude.

possessions

Two or three times Sonia's house is broken into while she is away. Whatever jewellery she has is stolen, and the silver, and a vase. This is a matter of course.

Germaine often gives her possessions away.

Jean is always losing things.

poverty

Jean knows what it is to be poor. She was once tempted to steal a collar which she could not afford from a Woolworth's.

Sonia understands that one might not be able to buy a suit, or shoes, or a winter coat.

Germaine often gives money to people so they can buy what she knows they can't afford.

publicity

Though she will not agree to being interviewed, Jean is enthusiastic about posing in designer clothes for the fashion section of the *Sunday Times*. In the black and white photographs, she appears dry, drawn, overly made up; she is unsmiling.

Sonia never refers to the use of her name in newspapers and magazines, not even to condemn the use.

Germaine says to me, "I don't care what you write about me. I can't care. So much has been written about me, and all of it is, as I'm sure what you've written is, wrong."

R

reading others' books

When you give one of your books, just published, to Jean, she looks at you sadly, as if you have just put some small, pathetic, dead pet into her hands, and she commiserates over its death.

Sonia, on receiving a new book from you, sends a lovely note to thank you; she never again mentions the book, though you're sure she has read it and passed on it a very severe judgement.

You give Germaine a copy of your book and say, "I don't want to know what you think of it," and she says, "Very well." You see it on her bedroom floor, among magazines and pantihose.

S

salvation

For Jean, it occurs, like fate, if it occurs at all, and it hardly matters what one does or doesn't do.

For Sonia, there is no salvation, not for anyone.

For Germaine, it is an act of will.

sex

If Jean is shy about sex, she is not anxious about it.

She has no vocabulary for it.

She tells me this (I'm not sure what the date of the incident is): "The only friend I made in France asked me to stay with her in the country for a weekend. To my real amazement her husband walked into my bedroom at night and obviously intended to get into bed with me. I mumbled something, How could I do it in Peggy's house? He took great offence at this and all the rest of my visit he was as rude as he could be. However, he drove me back to London, and after we had driven a little way he began to sing

'Our Miss Gibbs'. Of course I knew it by heart, and we sang all the way to London, and parted friends."

Sex is not terribly important.

Sonia often hints at past affairs. As she is, she herself says, a snob, the lovers were outstanding men, a painter, a writer, a philosopher. She refers often to the Israeli general.

She does not, I imagine, want anyone to say, "Sonia is fucked up because she's sexually unfulfilled." If sex is not, or never really was, important to her privately—or if she is and always was frightened of it—she suffers the importance she imagines the world gives it, the world of either sexual fulfilment or else neurosis. She could not bear anyone thinking she is sexually neurotic.

She says to me about a woman writer, "What she needs is a good lay."

"Sex," Germaine says to me, "is ninety per cent in the mind."

society

I ask a friend, thinking he would know, if the expression "going out into society" means anything today. His long face drawn longer as he thinks, he says, finally, "No," then thinks more and says, "Well, going to Sonia's."

Sonia instructs one on how to accept an invitation from an embassy.

She knows all about formal etiquette.

Jean does not, I think, belong to any "society".

Germaine does not seem to care about "society". In New York, at a party given for her to celebrate the success of *The Female Eunuch*, where people crowd about her to try to meet her, she spends the entire evening speaking to an Italian, and leaves saying to the hostess, simply, Thank you.

V

vocabulary

Germaine's vocabulary is vast. In describing a woman's illness, she uses the technical terms for all the parts of the body and their functions, as well as all the medical terms for the treatment. She would, in discussing drilling for oil or making bread or growing peonies, know all the technical terms.

In a conversation with Sonia, I notice she uses, over and over, what I imagine is a new word for her: "A man's putative writing . . ." "His putative moustache . . ."

Jean's vocabulary is small.

W

women

PORTRAIT OF A MARRIAGE

Nigel Nicolson

'A remarkable and superb book' *Spectator*

PORTRAIT OF A MARRIAGE tells the story of Harold
Nicolson's forty-nine-year marriage to Vita
Sackville-West, a union based on mutual trust, shared
interests, deepening love, total frankness and
reciprocal infidelity. It is also the journal of Vita's love
affair with Violet Trefusis, the crisis which nearly
broke the Nicolsons' unconventional but
extraordinarily successful marriage.

'Vita's . . . journal will earn an honoured place in the
records of confessional literature.' *The Times*

'Excels for intensity and unexpectedness anything of
its kind in fiction.' *Financial Times*

'Mr Nicolson's good faith is patent . . . the tone
perfect.' Sybille Bedford, *The Listener*

'The most convincing and enthralling of love stories.'
Economist

Futura Publications
Biography
0 8600 7091 3

All Futura Books are available at your bookshop or newsagent, or can be ordered from the following address:
Futura Books, Cash Sales Department,
P.O. Box 11, Falmouth, Cornwall.

Please send cheque or postal order (no currency), and allow 45p for postage and packing for the first book plus 20p for the second book and 14p for each additional book ordered up to a maximum charge of £1.63 in U.K.

Customers in Eire and B.F.P.O. please allow 45p for the first book, 20p for the second book plus 14p per copy for the next 7 books, thereafter 8p per book.

Overseas customers please allow 75p for postage and packing for the first book and 21p per copy for each additional book.